THE CATHOLIC BOOK OF SCRIPTURE PASSAGES

A PRAYER GUIDE FOR EVERY OCCASION

P9-CBQ-035

Compiled by Lucy Scholand

The Word Among Us Press
9639 Doctor Perry Road
Ijamsville, Maryland 21754
www.wordamongus.org

10 09 08 07 4 5 6 7

ISBN: 978-1-59325-061-4

Made and printed in the United States of America

Library of Congress Control Number: 2005929702

TABLE OF CONTENTS

INTRODUCTION

"All scripture is inspired by God and is useful for teaching, for reproof, for correction, and for training in righteousness, so that everyone who belongs to God may be proficient, equipped for every good work" (2 Timothy 3:16-17).

Paul might have added that Scripture is useful for prayer, but perhaps he thought this point needed no mention. The Bible is God's word of love to us. It naturally leads the human heart to praise, worship, and thanksgiving. Often I come to prayer feeling dry and distracted. Opening the Bible is an important step toward a fruitful time with the Lord. When I can't connect with God on my own, his word provides.

Moses, David, and "the cloud of witnesses" (Hebrews 12:1) God chose to put his word into writing were all human like us—in our weaknesses and in our desire to know our Lord and follow him ever more faithfully. Their thoughts often took the form of prayers that aptly express our own longing for him or need for his help, like this poetry from Psalm 63:1:

O God, you are my God, I seek you,
    my soul thirsts for you;
my flesh faints for you,
    as in a dry and weary land
        where there is no water.

What a blessing we have in making these words our own!

Wouldn't it be wonderful if the Bible were arranged by subject, so that you could easily turn to a Scripture verse or prayer to use in every situation? That's the purpose of this book: to give you words to pray for all the occasions in your life, whether you're celebrating the sacraments, interceding for others, or asking God for help in your own life. They are ancient words that have graced the lips of many Christians before you, divinely inspired words that are filled with life. I share with you in this book some of the riches I've gained through Scripture. My hope is that these Scripture passages will give you a deeper insight into Jesus' passion, death, and resurrection, as well as a greater appreciation of these sacred mysteries.

As Catholics, we are steeped in Scripture when we participate in the liturgical celebrations of our faith. We turn to the Scriptures at every Mass; the readings and the homilies that expound them can nourish us throughout the week. Liturgical music facilitates our familiarity with Scripture, as well, through hymns based on Scripture verses and beautifully arranged responsorial psalms. The psalms particularly came to mind as I prepared this book, and many of them are included here. Don't be surprised if you find yourself not just praying them but "singing" them to the familiar melodies you've heard at Mass.

The prayers in this book are divided into four sections. Since the sacraments are the pivotal moments in our lives as Catholics, I've begun with a section on Scripture and the sacraments. I've included prayers for all seven sacraments that can help you both in preparing to celebrate the sacraments and in deepening your understanding of them. For example, in the chapter on the Sacrament of Reconciliation, there are prayers to help you examine your conscience, express sorrow for your sins, make a sincere confession, and "go and sin no more." Sacramental prayers can be helpful at other times of life, as well. The Scripture passages associated with the anointing of the sick, for instance, can be used whenever you pray for healing. Scripture passages and prayers that touch on our sacramental life can also serve the practical purpose of providing the "right words" for these special events in the lives of our loved ones. How meaningful it can be to include a Scripture verse on a gift card for a wedding, ordination, baptism, first Communion, or confirmation!

Since the Mass is our celebration of the Eucharist, the chapter on the Eucharist contains prayers to use before and after Mass, as well as Scripture passages appropriate for meditating on the different parts of the Mass. And of course there are verses to pray after receiving Communion.

Through our celebration of the sacraments and the liturgy, we are united with one another and with the communion of saints—the body of Christ of which we are all members—which is the focus of the passages in Part II. Scripture provides a wealth of petitions we can use to intercede with Mary and the saints for the church as well as for all those who have gone before us in death. And since prayer is an opportunity for praise and thanksgiving as well as intercession, I've also included prayers here in honor of Mary, the saints, and the angels.

The third part of the book contains scriptural prayers we can offer for our own needs. Scripture shows us again and again that our concerns today are as old as mankind. If you face financial difficulties, for example, take heart: God loves the poor! I easily filled a chapter on God's provision, and I'm sure I did not exhaust all the references. There are also passages to help you pray for guidance, for help in relationships, and for freedom from worry, anxiety, and loneliness.

Finally, Part IV includes prayers for literally all times and seasons. There you'll find Scripture passages to pray at various times during the day, as well as verses that are particularly appropriate to the seasons of Advent, Christmas, Epiphany, Lent, Holy Week, Easter, and Pentecost. These scriptural prayers will help you make prayer and Scripture a regular part of your day as well as enrich your celebration of the Mass throughout the seasons of the liturgical year.

As I compiled this book of Bible passages, I've been amazed at how often the Old Testament words fit the New Testament realities of salvation. How true the saying of St. Augustine, who remarked, "The New Testament is hidden in the Old and the Old is made manifest in the New." For example, Mary's Magnificat (see Luke 1:46-56) is a medley of psalms—she really knew her Scripture! I find her response to Christ's presence in her womb to be a fitting prayer following our own reception of the body and blood of Christ. The Communion response for the Votive Mass of the Blessed Virgin confirms this: "Blessed is the womb of the Virgin Mary; she carried the Son of the eternal Father" (see Luke 11:27). So I have included the Magnificat among the prayers after Communion in Chapter 3 of this book, as well as among the prayers and Scripture verses honoring Mary in Chapter 10.

The Magnificat isn't the only Scripture passage that applies to more than one situation. Prayer doesn't come in neat compartments, and neither does Scripture. So rather than keep the reader paging back and forth to find other appropriate passages, I have included some of the most applicable prayers under more than one heading. However, when most of the Scripture passages in one chapter would also be appropriate for another topic, I have included a note to the reader instead. For instance, I have noted among the passages for Lent in Chapter 19 that additional prayers for repentance can be found in Chapter 4 on reconciliation. Passages on the Holy Spirit can be found in Chapter 2 on confirmation and also in Chapter 22 on Pentecost.

I'm sure that readers will find other inspirational words in Scripture, whether for celebrating the treasures of Catholic life or for seeking God's help in our daily lives. I know that I will continue to find words that could be included here. And that's the beauty of Scripture: it is an inexhaustible treasure. There is always more to discover. I consider well spent the hours of searching through the Bible and Catholic devotionals. What a rich and beautiful heritage we have in the Catholic Church! What a great God—kind, loving, and merciful! What a blessed Savior—Jesus Christ, our brother!

May this book of Scripture passages and prayers ignite your love of God's word, energize you to plumb its depths, and motivate you to return to it each day to drink of that "living water" who is Jesus, who is able to quench our thirst forever (John 4:10-14).

Lucy Scholand

PART ONE

SCRIPTURE AND THE SACRAMENTS

Christ himself is at work in the sacraments. Through them, we receive divine life. They are meant to bear fruit in our lives—and will bear fruit when our hearts are open and ready to encounter the Lord (*Catechism of the Catholic Church*, 1127-1131).

How can we prepare ourselves to receive the sacraments? Spending time in prayer with the Scripture verses here will help you understand more deeply the nature of the sacraments and their meaning for your life. Praying these passages will also give you expectant faith that through your reception of each sacrament, you will encounter Christ and that he will change you in that encounter.

These passages can also help you pray for others who are receiving a sacrament. Perhaps you know someone about to get married, ordained, or baptized into the church. You can pray these Scripture passages for them, or send them several verses as a "gift" before their big day.

We are truly a blessed people to be given the grace to partake in the sacramental life. As you pray through these Scripture passages, may you be filled with gratitude for all that Christ has done for us, and continues to do, through his church.

Chapter 1 | *Baptism*

In the beginning when God created the heavens and the earth, the earth was a formless void and darkness covered the face of the deep, while a wind from God swept over the face of the waters. (**Genesis 1:1-2**)

God waited patiently in the days of Noah, during the building of the ark, in which a few, that is, eight persons, were saved through water. And baptism, which this prefigured, now saves you—not as a removal of dirt from the body, but as an appeal to God for a good conscience, through the resurrection of Jesus Christ. (**1 Peter 3:20-21**)

Then Jesus came from Galilee to John at the Jordan, to be baptized by him. . . . And when Jesus had been baptized, just as he came up from the water, suddenly the heavens were opened to him and he saw the Spirit of God descending like a dove and alighting on him. And a voice from heaven said, "This is my Son, the Beloved, with whom I am well pleased." (**Matthew 3:13, 16-17**)

"Everyone who drinks of this water will be thirsty again, but those who drink of the water that I will give them will

never be thirsty. The water that I will give will become in them a spring of water gushing up to eternal life."
(John 4:13-14)

Washed Clean

Awake, awake,
    put on your strength, O Zion!
Put on your beautiful garments,
    O Jerusalem, the holy city;
for the uncircumcised and the unclean
    shall enter you no more.
Shake yourself from the dust, rise up,
    O captive Jerusalem;
loose the bonds from your neck,
    O captive daughter Zion!
For thus says the LORD: You were sold for nothing, and you shall be redeemed without money.
(Isaiah 52:1-3)

I have swept away your transgressions like a cloud,
    and your sins like mist;
return to me, for I have redeemed you.
Sing, O heavens, for the LORD has done it;
    shout, O depths of the earth;
break forth into singing, O mountains,
    O forest, and every tree in it!

For the LORD has redeemed Jacob,
   and will be glorified in Israel.
(Isaiah 44:22-23)

Blessed be the God and Father of our Lord Jesus Christ, who has blessed us in Christ with every spiritual blessing in the heavenly places, just as he chose us in Christ before the foundation of the world to be holy and blameless before him in love. He destined us for adoption as his children through Jesus Christ, according to the good pleasure of his will, to the praise of his glorious grace that he freely bestowed on us in the Beloved. In him we have redemption through his blood, the forgiveness of our trespasses, according to the riches of his grace that he lavished on us. (Ephesians 1:3-8)

So if anyone is in Christ, there is a new creation: everything old has passed away; see, everything has become new! All this is from God, who reconciled us to himself through Christ. (2 Corinthians 5:17-18)

All of us who have been baptized into Christ Jesus were baptized into his death. Therefore we have been buried with him by baptism into death, so that, just as Christ was raised from the dead by the glory of the Father, so we too might walk in newness of life. (Romans 6:3-4)

For once you were darkness, but now in the Lord you are light. Live as children of light—for the fruit of the light is found in all that is good and right and true.
(Ephesians 5:8-9)

Blessed are those who wash their robes, so that they will have the right to the tree of life and may enter the city by the gates. (Revelation 22:14)

God's Children

Is not he your father, who created you,
    who made you and established you?
(Deuteronomy 32:6)

"My faithfulness and steadfast love shall be with him;
    and in my name his horn shall be exalted.
I will set his hand on the sea
    and his right hand on the rivers.
He shall cry to me, 'You are my Father,
    my God, and the Rock of my salvation!'"
(Psalm 89:24-26)

Can a woman forget her nursing child,
    or show no compassion for the child of her womb?
Even these may forget,
    yet I will not forget you.

See, I have inscribed you on the palms of my hands. . . .
Then all flesh shall know
   that I am the LORD your Savior,
   and your Redeemer, the Mighty One of Jacob.
(Isaiah 49:15-16, 26)

He saved us, not because of any works of righteousness that we had done, but according to his mercy, through the water of rebirth and renewal by the Holy Spirit. This Spirit he poured out on us richly through Jesus Christ our Savior, so that, having been justified by his grace, we might become heirs according to the hope of eternal life.
(Titus 3:5-7)

We are the temple of the living God; as God said,
   "I will live in them and walk among them,
      and I will be their God,
      and they shall be my people.
   Therefore come out from them,
      and be separate from them, says the Lord,
   and touch nothing unclean;
      then I will welcome you,
   and I will be your father,
      and you shall be my sons and daughters,
   says the Lord Almighty."
(2 Corinthians 6:16-18)

"See, I am making all things new." . . . I am the Alpha and the Omega, the beginning and the end. To the thirsty I will give water as a gift from the spring of the water of life. Those who conquer will inherit these things, and I will be their God and they will be my children.
(Revelation 21:5-7)

We know that we are God's children, and that the whole world lies under the power of the evil one. And we know that the Son of God has come and has given us understanding so that we may know him who is true; and we are in him who is true, in his Son Jesus Christ. He is the true God and eternal life. (1 John 5:19-20)

When the fullness of time had come, God sent his Son, born of a woman, born under the law, in order to redeem those who were under the law, so that we might receive adoption as children. And because you are children, God has sent the Spirit of his Son into our hearts, crying, "Abba! Father!" So you are no longer a slave but a child, and if a child then also an heir, through God. (Galatians 4:4-7)

Called to Holiness

Come to him, a living stone, though rejected by mortals yet chosen and precious in God's sight, and like living stones, let yourselves be built into a spiritual house, to be a holy priesthood, to offer spiritual sacrifices acceptable to God through Jesus Christ. (**1 Peter 2:4-5**)

And all of us, with unveiled faces, seeing the glory of the Lord as though reflected in a mirror, are being transformed into the same image from one degree of glory to another; for this comes from the Lord, the Spirit.
(**2 Corinthians 3:18**)

You were taught to put away your former way of life, your old self, corrupt and deluded by its lusts, and to be renewed in the spirit of your minds, and to clothe yourselves with the new self, created according to the likeness of God in true righteousness and holiness. (**Ephesians 4:22-24**)

"For if you love those who love you, what reward do you have? Do not even the tax collectors do the same? And if you greet only your brothers and sisters, what more are you doing than others? Do not even the Gentiles do the same? Be perfect, therefore, as your heavenly Father is perfect." (**Matthew 5:46-48**)

You are a chosen race, a royal priesthood, a holy nation, God's own people, in order that you may proclaim the mighty acts of him who called you out of darkness into his marvelous light. (**1 Peter 2:9**)

Called to Serve

"Choose this day whom you will serve. . . . As for me and my household, we will serve the LORD." (**Joshua 24:15**)

> Gladden the soul of your servant,
>   for to you, O Lord, I lift up my soul.
> For you, O Lord, are good and forgiving,
>   abounding in steadfast love to all who call on you.
> (**Psalm 86:4-5**)

"You call me Teacher and Lord—and you are right, for that is what I am. So if I, your Lord and Teacher, have washed your feet, you also ought to wash one another's feet. For I have set you an example, that you also should do as I have done to you. Very truly, I tell you, servants are not greater than their master, nor are messengers greater than the one who sent them. If you know these things, you are blessed if you do them." (**John 13:13-17**)

"Who then is the faithful and wise slave, whom his master has put in charge of his household, to give the other slaves their allowance of food at the proper time? Blessed is that slave whom his master will find at work when he arrives. Truly I tell you, he will put that one in charge of all his possessions." (**Matthew 24:45-47**)

The greatest among you will be your servant. All who exalt themselves will be humbled, and all who humble themselves will be exalted. (**Matthew 23:11-12**)

"Whoever serves me must follow me, and where I am, there will my servant be also. Whoever serves me, the Father will honor." (**John 12:26**)

Chapter 2 | *Confirmation*

John answered all of them by saying, "I baptize you with water; but one who is more powerful than I is coming; I am not worthy to untie the thong of his sandals. He will baptize you with the Holy Spirit and fire." (**Luke 3:16**)

"Very truly, I tell you, no one can enter the kingdom of God without being born of water and Spirit. What is born of the flesh is flesh, and what is born of the Spirit is spirit. Do not be astonished that I said to you, 'You must be born from above.' The wind blows where it chooses, and you hear the sound of it, but you do not know where it comes from or where it goes. So it is with everyone who is born of the Spirit." (**John 3:5-8**)

The Spirit Comes

"I will ask the Father, and he will give you another Advocate, to be with you forever. This is the Spirit of truth, whom the world cannot receive, because it neither sees him nor knows him. You know him, because he abides with you, and he will be in you. . . .

"Those who love me will keep my word, and my Father will love them, and we will come to them and make our home with them. . . . The Advocate, the Holy Spirit, whom the Father will send in my name, will teach you everything, and remind you of all that I have said to you." (**John 14:16-18, 23, 26**)

> "See, the home of God is among mortals.
> He will dwell with them as their God;
> they will be his peoples,
> and God himself will be with them."
> (**Revelation 21:3**)

God's love has been poured into our hearts through the Holy Spirit that has been given to us. (**Romans 5:5**)

In him you also, when you had heard the word of truth, the gospel of your salvation, and had believed in him, were marked with the seal of the promised Holy Spirit;

this is the pledge of our inheritance toward redemption as God's own people, to the praise of his glory.
(Ephesians 1:13-14)

Gifts of the Spirit

The spirit of the LORD shall rest on him,
    the spirit of wisdom and understanding,
    the spirit of counsel and might,
    the spirit of knowledge and the fear of the LORD.
His delight shall be in the fear of the LORD.
(Isaiah 11:2-3)

You have dealt well with your servant,
    O LORD, according to your word.
Teach me good judgment and knowledge,
    for I believe in your commandments.
(Psalm 119:65-66)

The fear of the LORD is the beginning of wisdom;
    all those who practice it have a good
        understanding.
    His praise endures forever.
(Psalm 111:10)

Blessed be the name of God from age to age,
    for wisdom and power are his.

He changes times and seasons,
    deposes kings and sets up kings;
he gives wisdom to the wise
    and knowledge to those who have understanding.
He reveals deep and hidden things;
    he knows what is in the darkness,
    and light dwells with him.
To you, O God of my ancestors,
    I give thanks and praise,
for you have given me wisdom and power.
(Daniel 2:20-23)

There are varieties of gifts, but the same Spirit; and there are varieties of services, but the same Lord; and there are varieties of activities, but it is the same God who activates all of them in everyone. To each is given the manifestation of the Spirit for the common good.

To one is given through the Spirit the utterance of wisdom, and to another the utterance of knowledge according to the same Spirit, to another faith by the same Spirit, to another gifts of healing by the one Spirit, to another the working of miracles, to another prophecy, to another the discernment of spirits, to another various kinds of tongues, to another the interpretation of tongues. All these are activated by one and the same Spirit, who allots to each one individually just as the Spirit chooses.

For just as the body is one and has many members, and all the members of the body, though many, are one body, so it is with Christ. For in the one Spirit we were all baptized into one body—Jews or Greeks, slaves or free—and we were all made to drink of one Spirit. (**1 Corinthians 12:4-13**)

Hold to the standard of sound teaching that you have heard from me, in the faith and love that are in Christ Jesus. Guard the good treasure entrusted to you, with the help of the Holy Spirit living in us. (**2 Timothy 1:13-14**)

> "The Spirit of the Lord is upon me,
>   because he has anointed me
>   to bring good news to the poor.
> He has sent me to proclaim release to the captives
>   and recovery of sight to the blind,
>   to let the oppressed go free,
> to proclaim the year of the Lord's favor."
> (**Luke 4:18-19**)

If by the Spirit you put to death the deeds of the body, you will live. For all who are led by the Spirit of God are children of God. For you did not receive a spirit of slavery to fall back into fear, but you have received a spirit of adoption. When we cry, "Abba! Father!" it is that very Spirit bearing witness with our spirit that we are children of God, and if children, then heirs, heirs of God and joint heirs with Christ—if, in fact, we suffer with him so that we may also be glorified with him. (**Romans 8:13-17**)

Thanks be to God, who in Christ always leads us in triumphal procession, and through us spreads in every place the fragrance that comes from knowing him. For we are the aroma of Christ to God among those who are being saved and among those who are perishing. (**2 Corinthians 2:14-15**)

For the Confirmandi

I give thanks to my God always for you because of the grace of God that has been given you in Christ Jesus, for in every way you have been enriched in him, in speech and knowledge of every kind—just as the testimony of Christ has been strengthened among you—so that you are not lacking in any spiritual gift as you wait for the revealing of our Lord Jesus Christ. He will also strengthen you to the end, so that you may be blameless on the day of our Lord Jesus Christ. God is faithful; by him you were called into the fellowship of his Son, Jesus Christ our Lord. (**1 Corinthians 1:4-9**)

Like newborn infants, long for the pure, spiritual milk, so that by it you may grow into salvation—if indeed you have tasted that the Lord is good. (**1 Peter 2:2-3**)

Do not quench the Spirit. Do not despise the words of prophets, but test everything; hold fast to what is good;

abstain from every form of evil.

May the God of peace himself sanctify you entirely; and may your spirit and soul and body be kept sound and blameless at the coming of our Lord Jesus Christ. The one who calls you is faithful, and he will do this.

Beloved, pray for us. (**1 Thessalonians 5:19-25**)

"You are the salt of the earth; but if salt has lost its taste, how can its saltiness be restored? It is no longer good for anything, but is thrown out and trampled under foot.

"You are the light of the world. A city built on a hill cannot be hid. No one after lighting a lamp puts it under the bushel basket, but on the lampstand, and it gives light to all in the house. In the same way, let your light shine before others, so that they may see your good works and give glory to your Father in heaven." (**Matthew 5:13-16**)

You then, my child, be strong in the grace that is in Christ Jesus. (**2 Timothy 2:1**)

Chapter 3 | *The Eucharist*

On this mountain the LORD of hosts will make
    for all peoples
  a feast of rich food, a feast of well-aged wines,
  of rich food filled with marrow,
    of well-aged wines strained clear.

And he will destroy on this mountain
>> the shroud that is cast over all peoples,
>> the sheet that is spread over all nations;
>> he will swallow up death forever.
> Then the Lord GOD will wipe away the tears
>> from all faces,
>> and the disgrace of his people he will take away
>> from all the earth,
>> for the LORD has spoken.
> It will be said on that day,
>> Lo, this is our God; we have waited for him, so
>> that he might save us.
>> This is the LORD for whom we have waited;
>> let us be glad and rejoice in his salvation.

(Isaiah 25:6-9)

"I am the bread of life. Whoever comes to me will never be hungry, and whoever believes in me will never be thirsty. . . . Very truly, I tell you, whoever believes has eternal life. I am the bread of life. Your ancestors ate the manna in the wilderness, and they died. This is the bread that comes down from heaven, so that one may eat of it and not die. I am the living bread that came down from heaven. Whoever eats of this bread will live forever; and the bread that I will give for the life of the world is my flesh." **(John 6:35, 47-51)**

"Do not work for the food that perishes, but for the food that endures for eternal life, which the Son of Man will give you. For it is on him that God the Father has set his seal." (**John 6:27**)

Adoration before the Blessed Sacrament

I, through the abundance of your steadfast love,
   will enter your house,
I will bow down toward your holy temple
   in awe of you.
(**Psalm 5:7**)

How lovely is your dwelling place,
   O LORD of hosts!
My soul longs, indeed it faints
   for the courts of the LORD;
my heart and my flesh sing for joy
   to the living God.
(**Psalm 84:1-2**)

"Come," my heart says, "seek his face!"
   Your face, LORD, do I seek.
(**Psalm 27:8**)

O come, let us sing to the LORD;
   let us make a joyful noise to the rock

of our salvation!
Let us come into his presence with thanksgiving;
   let us make a joyful noise to him
      with songs of praise!
For the LORD is a great God,
   and a great King above all gods.
In his hand are the depths of the earth;
   the heights of the mountains are his also.
The sea is his, for he made it,
   and the dry land, which his hands have formed.
O come, let us worship and bow down,
   let us kneel before the LORD, our Maker!
For he is our God,
   and we are the people of his pasture,
   and the sheep of his hand.
(Psalm 95:1-7a)

Praise the LORD!
Sing to the LORD a new song,
   his praise in the assembly of the faithful.
Let Israel be glad in its Maker;
   let the children of Zion rejoice in their King.
Let them praise his name with dancing,
   making melody to him with tambourine and lyre.
For the LORD takes pleasure in his people;
   he adorns the humble with victory.
Let the faithful exult in glory;

let them sing for joy on their couches.
Let the high praises of God be in their throats.
(**Psalm 149:1-6a**)

Now to him who is able to keep you from falling, and to make you stand without blemish in the presence of his glory with rejoicing, to the only God our Savior, through Jesus Christ our Lord, be glory, majesty, power, and authority, before all time and now and forever. Amen. (**Jude 1:24-25**)

Before Mass

So when you are offering your gift at the altar, if you remember that your brother or sister has something against you, leave your gift there before the altar and go; first be reconciled to your brother or sister, and then come and offer your gift. (**Matthew 5:23-24**)

"Have mercy on us, Lord, Son of David!"
(**Matthew 20:31**)

Then Jesus said to him, "Someone gave a great dinner and invited many. At the time for the dinner he sent his slave to say to those who had been invited, 'Come; for everything is ready now.' But they all alike began to make excuses. . . . Then the owner of the house became angry and said to his slave, 'Go out at once into the streets and lanes of the town and bring in the poor, the crippled, the blind, and the lame.' And the slave said, 'Sir, what you ordered has been done, and there is still room.' Then the master said to the slave, 'Go out into the roads and lanes, and compel people to come in, so that my house may be filled.'" (Luke 14:16-18, 21-23)

The Liturgy of the Word

O that today you would listen to his voice!
(Psalm 95:7b)

"Come, let us go up to the mountain of the LORD,
    to the house of the God of Jacob;
that he may teach us his ways
    and that we may walk in his paths."
For out of Zion shall go forth instruction,
    and the word of the LORD from Jerusalem.
(Isaiah 2:3)

I treasure your word in my heart,
    so that I may not sin against you.
Blessed are you, O LORD;
    teach me your statutes.
With my lips I declare
    all the ordinances of your mouth.

I delight in the way of your decrees
    as much as in all riches.
I will meditate on your precepts,
    and fix my eyes on your ways.
I will delight in your statutes;
    I will not forget your word. . . .
Open my eyes, so that I may behold
    wondrous things out of your law.
(Psalm 119:11-16, 18)

How sweet are your words to my taste,
    sweeter than honey to my mouth!
Through your precepts I get understanding;
    therefore I hate every false way.
Your word is a lamp to my feet
    and a light to my path.
(Psalm 119:103-105)

Indeed, the word of God is living and active, sharper than any two-edged sword, piercing until it divides soul from spirit, joints from marrow; it is able to judge the thoughts and intentions of the heart. **(Hebrews 4:12)**

The Liturgy of the Eucharist

"Our Father in heaven,
    hallowed be your name.

Your kingdom come.
Your will be done,
    on earth as it is in heaven.
Give us this day our daily bread.
And forgive us our debts,
    as we also have forgiven our debtors.
And do not bring us to the time of trial,
    but rescue us from the evil one."
(Matthew 6:9-13)

You prepare a table before me. . . .
Surely goodness and mercy shall follow me
    all the days of my life,
and I shall dwell in the house of the LORD
    my whole life long.
(Psalm 23:5-6)

While they were eating, Jesus took a loaf of bread, and after blessing it he broke it, gave it to the disciples, and said, "Take, eat; this is my body." Then he took a cup, and after giving thanks he gave it to them, saying, "Drink from it, all of you; for this is my blood of the covenant, which is poured out for many for the forgiveness of sins. I tell you, I will never again drink of this fruit of the vine until that day when I drink it new with you in my Father's kingdom." **(Matthew 26:26-29)**

For as often as you eat this bread and drink the cup, you proclaim the Lord's death until he comes.
(1 Corinthians 11:26)

"Here is the Lamb of God who takes away the sin of the world!"(John 1:29)

"Lord, . . . I am not worthy to have you come under my roof. . . . But only speak the word, and let my servant be healed." (Luke 7:6-7)

The cup of blessing that we bless, is it not a sharing in the blood of Christ? The bread that we break, is it not a sharing in the body of Christ? Because there is one bread, we who are many are one body, for we all partake of the one bread. (1 Corinthians 10:16-17)

"Those who eat my flesh and drink my blood have eternal life, and I will raise them up on the last day; for my flesh is true food and my blood is true drink. Those who eat my flesh and drink my blood abide in me, and I in them. Just as the living Father sent me, and I live because of the Father, so whoever eats me will live because of me. This is the bread that came down from heaven, not like that which your ancestors ate, and they died. But the one who eats this bread will live forever." (John 6:54-58)

After Communion

He brought me to the banqueting house,
    and his intention toward me was love.
(Song of Solomon 2:4)

[Lord,] I am continually with you;
    you hold my right hand.
You guide me with your counsel,
    and afterward you will receive me with honor.
Whom have I in heaven but you?
    And there is nothing on earth that I desire
        other than you.
My flesh and my heart may fail,
    but God is the strength of my heart
        and my portion forever. . . .
For me it is good to be near God;
    I have made the Lord God my refuge,
    to tell of all your works.
(Psalm 73:23-26, 28)

O taste and see that the Lord is good;
    happy are those who take refuge in him.
(Psalm 34:8)

"Peace be with you. As the Father has sent me, so I send you." (John 20:21)

It is no longer I who live, but it is Christ who lives in me.
And the life I now live in the flesh I live by faith in the Son
of God, who loved me and gave himself for me.
(**Galatians 2:20**)

"My soul magnifies the Lord,
   and my spirit rejoices in God my Savior,
for he has looked with favor on the lowliness
      of his servant.
   Surely, from now on all generations will
      call me blessed;
for the Mighty One has done great things for me,
   and holy is his name.
His mercy is for those who fear him
   from generation to generation.
He has shown strength with his arm;
   he has scattered the proud in the thoughts
      of their hearts.
He has brought down the powerful from their thrones,
   and lifted up the lowly;
he has filled the hungry with good things,
   and sent the rich away empty.
He has helped his servant Israel,
   in remembrance of his mercy,
according to the promise he made to our ancestors,
   to Abraham and to his descendants forever."
(**Luke 1:46-55**)

Chapter 4 | *Reconciliation*

"Those who are well have no need of a physician, but those who are sick; I have come to call not the righteous but sinners to repentance." (**Luke 5:31-32**)

"I tell you, there will be more joy in heaven over one sinner who repents than over ninety-nine righteous persons who need no repentance." (**Luke 15:7**)

"We had to celebrate and rejoice, because this brother of yours was dead and has come to life; he was lost and has been found." (**Luke 15:32**)

In Christ God was reconciling the world to himself, not counting their trespasses against them, and entrusting the message of reconciliation to us. So we are ambassadors for Christ, since God is making his appeal through us; we entreat you on behalf of Christ, be reconciled to God. (**2 Corinthians 5:19-20**)

Examination of Conscience

I am the LORD your God, who brought you out of the land of Egypt, out of the house of slavery; you shall have no other gods before me. . . .

You shall not make wrongful use of the name of the LORD your God. . . .

Remember the sabbath day, and keep it holy. . . .

Honor your father and your mother. . . .

You shall not murder.

You shall not commit adultery.

You shall not steal.

You shall not bear false witness against your neighbor.

You shall not covet your neighbor's house; you shall not covet your neighbor's wife . . . or anything that belongs to your neighbor. (**Exodus 20:2, 7, 8, 12, 13-17**)

Search me, O God, and know my heart;
    test me and know my thoughts.
See if there is any wicked way in me,
    and lead me in the way everlasting.
(**Psalm 139:23-24**)

I have gone astray like a lost sheep;
    seek out your servant,
        for I do not forget your commandments.
(**Psalm 119:176**)

"You have heard that it was said to those of ancient times, 'You shall not murder'; and 'whoever murders shall be liable to judgment.' But I say to you that if you are angry with a brother or sister, you will be liable to judgment; and if you insult a brother or sister, you will be liable to the council; and if you say, 'You fool,' you will be liable to the hell of fire." (**Matthew 5:21-22**)

"No good tree bears bad fruit, nor again does a bad tree bear good fruit; for each tree is known by its own fruit. Figs are not gathered from thorns, nor are grapes picked from a bramble bush. The good person out of the good treasure of the heart produces good, and the evil person out of evil treasure produces evil; for it is out of the abundance of the heart that the mouth speaks."
(**Luke 6:43-45**)

"You have heard that it was said, 'You shall love your neighbor and hate your enemy.' But I say to you, Love your enemies and pray for those who persecute you, so that you may be children of your Father in heaven; for he makes his sun rise on the evil and on the good, and sends rain on the righteous and on the unrighteous. . . . Be perfect, therefore, as your heavenly Father is perfect."
(**Matthew 5:43-45, 48**)

Sorrow for Our Sins

"Father, I have sinned against heaven and before you; I am no longer worthy to be called your son."
(**Luke 15:21**)

Have mercy on me, O God,
    according to your steadfast love;
according to your abundant mercy
    blot out my transgressions.
Wash me thoroughly from my iniquity,
    and cleanse me from my sin.
For I know my transgressions,
    and my sin is ever before me. . . .
You desire truth in the inward being;
    therefore teach me wisdom in my secret heart.
Purge me with hyssop, and I shall be clean;
    wash me, and I shall be whiter than snow.
Let me hear joy and gladness;
    let the bones that you have crushed rejoice.
Hide your face from my sins,
    and blot out all my iniquities.
Create in me a clean heart, O God,
    and put a new and right spirit within me.
Do not cast me away from your presence,
    and do not take your holy spirit from me.
Restore to me the joy of your salvation,
    and sustain in me a willing spirit. . . .
O Lord, open my lips,
    and my mouth will declare your praise.
For you have no delight in sacrifice;
    if I were to give a burnt offering,
        you would not be pleased.
The sacrifice acceptable to God is a broken spirit;

a broken and contrite heart, O God,
    you will not despise.
(Psalm 51:1-3, 6-12, 15-17)

Out of the depths I cry to you, O LORD.
    Lord, hear my voice!
Let your ears be attentive
    to the voice of my supplications!
If you, O LORD, should mark iniquities,
    Lord, who could stand?
But there is forgiveness with you,
    so that you may be revered. . . .
O Israel, hope in the LORD!
    For with the LORD there is steadfast love,
    and with him is great power to redeem.
It is he who will redeem Israel
    from all its iniquities.
(Psalm 130:1-4, 7-8)

While I kept silence, my body wasted away
    through my groaning all day long.
For day and night your hand was heavy upon me;
    my strength was dried up as by the heat
        of summer.
Then I acknowledged my sin to you,
    and I did not hide my iniquity;
I said, "I will confess my transgressions to the LORD,"
    and you forgave the guilt of my sin.

Therefore let all who are faithful
    offer prayer to you;
at a time of distress, the rush of mighty waters
    shall not reach them.
You are a hiding place for me;
    you preserve me from trouble;
    you surround me with glad cries of deliverance.
(Psalm 32:3-7)

To you, O Lord, I lift up my soul.
O my God, in you I trust; . . .
Be mindful of your mercy, O Lord,
        and of your steadfast love,
    for they have been from of old.
Do not remember the sins of my youth
        or my transgressions;
    according to your steadfast love remember me,
    for your goodness' sake, O Lord!
Good and upright is the Lord;
    therefore he instructs sinners in the way.
He leads the humble in what is right,
    and teaches the humble his way.
All the paths of the Lord are steadfast love
        and faithfulness,
    for those who keep his covenant and his decrees.
For your name's sake, O Lord,
    pardon my guilt, for it is great. . . .
Turn to me and be gracious to me,

for I am lonely and afflicted.
Relieve the troubles of my heart,
	and bring me out of my distress.
Consider my affliction and my trouble,
	and forgive all my sins.
(Psalm 25:1-2a, 6-11, 16-18)

"God, be merciful to me, a sinner!" **(Luke 18:13)**

Go and Sin No More

Stand at the crossroads, and look,
	and ask for the ancient paths,
where the good way lies; and walk in it,
	and find rest for your souls.
(Jeremiah 6:16)

Teach me your way, O LORD,
	and lead me on a level path.
(Psalm 27:11)

Before I was humbled I went astray,
	but now I keep your word.
You are good and do good;
	teach me your statutes. . . .
With my whole heart I keep your precepts. . . .
	I delight in your law.

It is good for me that I was humbled,
    so that I might learn your statutes. . . .
My tongue will sing of your promise,
    for all your commandments are right.
Let your hand be ready to help me,
    for I have chosen your precepts.
I long for your salvation, O LORD,
    and your law is my delight.
Let me live that I may praise you,
    and let your ordinances help me.
(Psalm 119:67-71, 172-175)

"I will guard my ways
    that I may not sin with my tongue;
I will keep a muzzle on my mouth."
(Psalm 39:1)

Set a guard over my mouth, O LORD;
    keep watch over the door of my lips.
Do not turn my heart to any evil,
    to busy myself with wicked deeds
in company with those who work iniquity;
    do not let me eat of their delicacies.
Let the righteous strike me;
    let the faithful correct me.
Never let the oil of the wicked anoint my head. . . .
But my eyes are turned toward you, O GOD, my Lord;
    in you I seek refuge; do not leave me defenseless.

Keep me from the trap that they have laid for me,
   and from the snares of evildoers.
(Psalm 141:3-5, 8-9)

Vindicate me, O LORD,
   for I have walked in my integrity,
   and I have trusted in the LORD without wavering.
Prove me, O LORD, and try me;
   test my heart and mind.
For your steadfast love is before my eyes,
   and I walk in faithfulness to you.
(Psalm 26:1-3)

God, who is rich in mercy, out of the great love with which he loved us even when we were dead through our trespasses, made us alive together with Christ—by grace you have been saved—and raised us up with him and seated us with him in the heavenly places in Christ Jesus, so that in the ages to come he might show the immeasurable riches of his grace in kindness toward us in Christ Jesus. For by grace you have been saved through faith, and this is not your own doing; it is the gift of God—not the result of works, so that no one may boast. (Ephesians 2:4-9)

Chapter 5 | *The Anointing of the Sick*

Are any among you suffering? They should pray. Are any cheerful? They should sing songs of praise. Are any among you sick? They should call for the elders of the church and have them pray over them, anointing them with oil in the name of the Lord. The prayer of faith will save the sick, and the Lord will raise them up; and anyone who has committed sins will be forgiven. Therefore confess your sins to one another, and pray for one another, so that you may be healed. (James 5:13-16)

For Healing

"What joy is left for me any more? I am a man without eyesight; I cannot see the light of heaven, but I lie in darkness like the dead who no longer see the light. Although still alive, I am among the dead. I hear people but I cannot see them." But the young man said, "Take courage; the time is near for God to heal you; take courage." (Tobit 5:10)

> O LORD, do not rebuke me in your anger,
>   or discipline me in your wrath.
> Be gracious to me, O LORD, for I am languishing;
>   O LORD, heal me, for my bones are shaking
>   with terror.

My soul also is struck with terror,
      while you, O LORD—how long?
Turn, O LORD, save my life;
      deliver me for the sake of your steadfast love.
For in death there is no remembrance of you;
      in Sheol who can give you praise?
I am weary with my moaning;
      every night I flood my bed with tears;
      I drench my couch with my weeping.
My eyes waste away because of grief;
      they grow weak because of all my foes.
Depart from me, all you workers of evil,
      for the LORD has heard the sound of my weeping.
The LORD has heard my supplication;
      the LORD accepts my prayer.
(Psalm 6:1-9)

In you, O LORD, I seek refuge;
      do not let me ever be put to shame;
      in your righteousness deliver me.
Incline your ear to me;
      rescue me speedily.
Be a rock of refuge for me,
      a strong fortress to save me.
You are indeed my rock and my fortress;
      for your name's sake lead me and guide me,
take me out of the net that is hidden for me,
      for you are my refuge.

Into your hand I commit my spirit;
 you have redeemed me, O LORD, faithful GOD. . . .
 I have become like a broken vessel. . . .
But I trust in you, O LORD;
 I say, "You are my God."
My times are in your hand; . . .
Let your face shine upon your servant;
 save me in your steadfast love.
(Psalm 31:1-5, 12, 14-16)

To you, O LORD, I cried,
 and to the LORD I made supplication:
"What profit is there in my death,
 if I go down to the Pit?
Will the dust praise you?
 Will it tell of your faithfulness?
Hear, O LORD, and be gracious to me!
 O LORD, be my helper!"
You have turned my mourning into dancing;
 you have taken off my sackcloth
 and clothed me with joy,
so that my soul may praise you and not be silent.
 O LORD my God, I will give thanks to you forever.
(Psalm 30:8-12)

"If I but touch his clothes, I will be made well."
(Mark 5:28)

Once, when he was in one of the cities, there was a man covered with leprosy. When he saw Jesus, he bowed with his face to the ground and begged him, "Lord, if you choose, you can make me clean." Then Jesus stretched out his hand, touched him, and said, "I do choose. Be made clean." Immediately the leprosy left him. (**Luke 5:12-13**)

That evening they brought to [Jesus] many who were possessed with demons; and he cast out the spirits with a word, and cured all who were sick. This was to fulfill what had been spoken through the prophet Isaiah, "He took our infirmities and bore our diseases." (**Matthew 8:16-17**)

Jesus had just then cured many people of diseases, plagues, and evil spirits, and had given sight to many who were blind. And he answered them, "Go and tell John what you have seen and heard: the blind receive their sight, the lame walk, the lepers are cleansed, the deaf hear, the dead are raised, the poor have good news brought to them. And blessed is anyone who takes no offense at me." (**Luke 7:21-23**)

Trust in God

We can say with confidence, "The Lord is my helper; I will not be afraid." (**Hebrews 13:6**)

O Most High, when I am afraid,
    I put my trust in you.
In God, whose word I praise,
    in God I trust; I am not afraid.
(Psalm 56:2-4)

How precious is your steadfast love, O God!
    All people may take refuge in
        the shadow of your wings.
They feast on the abundance of your house,
    and you give them drink
        from the river of your delights.
For with you is the fountain of life;
    in your light we see light.
O continue your steadfast love
        to those who know you,
    and your salvation to the upright of heart!
(Psalm 36:7-10)

Those of steadfast mind you keep in peace—
    in peace because they trust in you.
Trust in the LORD forever,
    for in the LORD GOD
        you have an everlasting rock.
(Isaiah 26:3-4)

I am convinced that neither death, nor life, nor angels, nor rulers, nor things present, nor things to come, nor powers, nor height, nor depth, nor anything else in all creation, will be able to separate us from the love of God in Christ Jesus our Lord. (**Romans 8:38-39**)

"If you are able to do anything, have pity on us and help us." Jesus said to him, "If you are able!—All things can be done for the one who believes." Immediately the father of the child cried out, "I believe; help my unbelief!" (**Mark 9:22-24**)

Thanksgiving for Healing

Blessed be the LORD,
  for he has heard the sound of my pleadings.
The LORD is my strength and my shield;
  in him my heart trusts;
so I am helped, and my heart exults,
  and with my song I give thanks to him.
The LORD is the strength of his people;
  he is the saving refuge of his anointed.
O save your people, and bless your heritage;
  be their shepherd, and carry them forever.
(**Psalm 28:6-9**)

Some were sick through their sinful ways,
    and because of their iniquities endured affliction;
they loathed any kind of food,
    and they drew near to the gates of death.
Then they cried to the LORD in their trouble,
    and he saved them from their distress;
he sent out his word and healed them,
    and delivered them from destruction.
Let them thank the LORD for his steadfast love,
    for his wonderful works to humankind.
And let them offer thanksgiving sacrifices,
    and tell of his deeds with songs of joy.
(Psalm 107:17-22)

You who fear the LORD, praise him!
    All you offspring of Jacob, glorify him;
    stand in awe of him, all you offspring of Israel!
For he did not despise or abhor
    the affliction of the afflicted;
he did not hide his face from me,
    but heard when I cried to him.
(Psalm 22:23-24)

I am like a green olive tree
    in the house of God.
I trust in the steadfast love of God
    forever and ever.
I will thank you forever,

because of what you have done.
In the presence of the faithful
I will proclaim your name, for it is good.
(Psalm 52:8-9)

For the Dying

The LORD is my shepherd, I shall not want.
He makes me lie down in green pastures;
he leads me beside still waters;
he restores my soul.
He leads me in right paths
for his name's sake.
Even though I walk through the darkest valley,
I fear no evil;
for you are with me;
your rod and your staff—
they comfort me.
You prepare a table before me
in the presence of my enemies;
you anoint my head with oil;
my cup overflows.
Surely goodness and mercy shall follow me
all the days of my life,
and I shall dwell in the house of the LORD
my whole life long.
(Psalm 23)

"Master, now you are dismissing
        your servant in peace,
    according to your word;
for my eyes have seen your salvation,
    which you have prepared in the presence
        of all peoples,
a light for revelation to the Gentiles
    and for glory to your people Israel." (**Luke 2:29-32**)

As for me, I am already being poured out as a libation, and the time of my departure has come. I have fought the good fight, I have finished the race, I have kept the faith. From now on there is reserved for me the crown of righteousness, which the Lord, the righteous judge, will give me on that day, and not only to me but also to all who have longed for his appearing. (**2 Timothy 4:6-8**)

This perishable body must put on imperishability, and this mortal body must put on immortality. When this perishable body puts on imperishability, and this mortal body puts on immortality, then the saying that is written will be fulfilled:
    "Death has been swallowed up in victory."
    "Where, O death, is your victory?
        Where, O death, is your sting?"
The sting of death is sin, and the power of sin is the law. But thanks be to God, who gives us the victory through our Lord Jesus Christ. (**1 Corinthians 15:53-57**)

Therefore we have been buried with him by baptism into death, so that, just as Christ was raised from the dead by the glory of the Father, so we too might walk in newness of life.

For if we have been united with him in a death like his, we will certainly be united with him in a resurrection like his. (Romans 6:4-5)

Jesus said to her, "I am the resurrection and the life. Those who believe in me, though they die, will live, and everyone who lives and believes in me will never die." (John 11:25-26)

"Father, into your hands I commend my spirit." (Luke 23:46)

"Lord Jesus, receive my spirit." (Acts 7:59)

Chapter 6 | *Holy Orders*

The gifts he gave were that some would be apostles, some prophets, some evangelists, some pastors and teachers, to equip the saints for the work of ministry, for building up the body of Christ, until all of us come to the unity of the faith and of the knowledge of the Son of God, to maturity, to the measure of the full stature of Christ. (Ephesians 4:11-13)

The Mission of the Priesthood

King Melchizedek of Salem brought out bread and wine; he was priest of God Most High. He blessed [Abram] and said,

"Blessed be Abram by God Most High,
    maker of heaven and earth;
and blessed be God Most High." (**Genesis 14:18-20**)

So Moses went out and told the people the words of the LORD; and he gathered seventy elders of the people, and placed them all around the tent. Then the LORD came down in the cloud and spoke to him, and took some of the spirit that was on him and put it on the seventy elders; and when the spirit rested upon them, they prophesied. (**Numbers 11:24-25**)

"You are a priest forever according
    to the order of Melchizedek."
(**Psalm 110:4**)

We have such a high priest, one who is seated at the right hand of the throne of the Majesty in the heavens, a minister in the sanctuary and the true tent that the Lord, and not any mortal, has set up. . . . Jesus has now obtained a more excellent ministry, and to that degree he is the mediator of a better covenant, which has been enacted through better promises. (**Hebrews 8:1-2, 6**)

For I received from the Lord what I also handed on to you, that the Lord Jesus on the night when he was betrayed took a loaf of bread, and when he had given thanks, he broke it and said, "This is my body that is for you. Do this in remembrance of me." In the same way he took the cup also, after supper, saying, "This cup is the new covenant in my blood. Do this, as often as you drink it, in remembrance of me." For as often as you eat this bread and drink the cup, you proclaim the Lord's death until he comes. (**1 Corinthians 11:23-26**)

Called to Preach

How beautiful upon the mountains
    are the feet of the messenger
        who announces peace,
who brings good news,
    who announces salvation,
        who says to Zion, "Your God reigns."
(**Isaiah 52:7**)

The lips of a priest should guard knowledge, and people should seek instruction from his mouth, for he is the messenger of the LORD of hosts. (**Malachi 2:7**)

There is one God;
    there is also one mediator
      between God and humankind,
Christ Jesus, himself human,
    who gave himself a ransom for all
—this was attested at the right time. For this I was appointed a herald and an apostle. (**1 Timothy 2:5-7**)

Pray . . . for me, so that when I speak, a message may be given to me to make known with boldness the mystery of the gospel, for which I am an ambassador in chains. Pray that I may declare it boldly, as I must speak.
(**Ephesians 6:19-20**)

In the presence of God and of Christ Jesus, who is to judge the living and the dead, and in view of his appearing and his kingdom, I solemnly urge you: proclaim the message; be persistent whether the time is favorable or unfavorable; convince, rebuke, and encourage, with the utmost patience in teaching. For the time is coming when people will not put up with sound doctrine, but having itching ears, they will accumulate for themselves teachers to suit their own desires, and will turn away from listening to the truth and wander away to myths. As for you, always be sober, endure suffering, do the work of an evangelist, carry out your ministry fully. (**2 Timothy 4:1-5**)

Called to Pastor God's People

O LORD my God, . . . your servant is in the midst of the people whom you have chosen. . . . Give your servant therefore an understanding mind to govern your people, able to discern between good and evil. (**1 Kings 3:7-9**)

Now as an elder myself and a witness of the sufferings of Christ, as well as one who shares in the glory to be revealed, I exhort the elders among you to tend the flock of God that is in your charge, exercising the oversight, not under compulsion but willingly, as God would have you do it—not for sordid gain but eagerly. Do not lord it over those in your charge, but be examples to the flock. And when the chief shepherd appears, you will win the crown of glory that never fades away. (**1 Peter 5:1-4**)

For the grace of God has appeared, bringing salvation to all, training us to renounce impiety and worldly passions, and in the present age to live lives that are self-controlled, upright, and godly, while we wait for the blessed hope and the manifestation of the glory of our great God and Savior, Jesus Christ. He it is who gave himself for us that he might redeem us from all iniquity and purify for himself a people of his own who are zealous for good deeds. Declare these things; exhort and reprove with all authority. (**Titus 2:11-15**)

Do not neglect the gift that is in you, which was given to you through prophecy with the laying on of hands by the council of elders. Put these things into practice, devote yourself to them, so that all may see your progress. Pay close attention to yourself and to your teaching; continue in these things, for in doing this you will save both yourself and your hearers. (**1 Timothy 4:14-16**)

Deacons likewise must be serious, not double-tongued, not indulging in much wine, not greedy for money; they must hold fast to the mystery of the faith with a clear conscience. . . . Those who serve well as deacons gain a good standing for themselves and great boldness in the faith that is in Christ Jesus. (**1 Timothy 3:8-9, 13**)

Chapter 7 | *Matrimony*

So God created humankind in his image,
    in the image of God he created them;
    male and female he created them.
God blessed them, and God said to them, "Be fruitful and multiply, and fill the earth and subdue it." (**Genesis 1:27-28**)

Let marriage be held in honor by all. (**Hebrews 13:4**)

The man said,
> "This at last is bone of my bones
>> and flesh of my flesh;
> this one shall be called Woman,
>> for out of Man this one was taken."

Therefore a man leaves his father and his mother and clings to his wife, and they become one flesh. And the man and his wife were both naked, and were not ashamed. **(Genesis 2:23-25)**

> My beloved is mine and I am his;
>> he pastures his flock among the lilies.
> Until the day breathes
>> and the shadows flee.
> turn, my beloved, be like a gazelle
>> or a young stag on the cleft mountains.

(Song of Solomon 2:16-17)

Christ and His Bride

> I will greatly rejoice in the LORD,
>> my whole being shall exult in my God;
> for he has clothed me with the garments of salvation,
>> he has covered me with the robe of righteousness,
> as a bridegroom decks himself with a garland,
>> and as a bride adorns herself with her jewels.
> For as the earth brings forth its shoots,

and as a garden causes what is sown in it
    to spring up,
so the Lord God will cause righteousness and praise
    to spring up before all the nations.
(Isaiah 61:10-11)

Be imitators of God, as beloved children, and live in love, as Christ loved us and gave himself up for us, a fragrant offering and sacrifice to God. **(Ephesians 5:1-2)**

Be subject to one another out of reverence for Christ.
    Wives, be subject to your husbands as you are to the Lord. . . . Husbands, love your wives, just as Christ loved the church and gave himself up for her, in order to make her holy by cleansing her with the washing of water by the word, so as to present the church to himself in splendor, without a spot or wrinkle or anything of the kind—yes, so that she may be holy and without blemish. . . . He who loves his wife loves himself. For no one ever hates his own body, but he nourishes and tenderly cares for it, just as Christ does for the church, because we are members of his body. "For this reason a man will leave his father and mother and be joined to his wife, and the two will become one flesh." This is a great mystery, and I am applying it to Christ and the church. Each of you, however, should love his wife as himself, and a wife should respect her husband. **(Ephesians 5:21-22, 25-33)**

"Hallelujah!
For the Lord our God
    the Almighty reigns.
Let us rejoice and exult
    and give him the glory,
for the marriage of the Lamb has come,
    and his bride has made herself ready;
to her it has been granted to be clothed
    with fine linen, bright and pure"—
for the fine linen is the righteous deeds of the saints.
    And the angel said to me, "Write this: Blessed are
those who are invited to the marriage supper of the
Lamb." (Revelation 19:6-9)

A Husband's Prayer

"Blessed are you, O God of our ancestors,
    and blessed is your name in all generations forever.
Let the heavens and the whole creation
        bless you forever.
You made Adam, and for him you made his wife Eve
    as a helper and support.
    From the two of them the human race has sprung.
You said, 'It is not good that the man should be alone;
    let us make a helper for him like himself.'
I now am taking this kinswoman of mine,

not because of lust,
but with sincerity.
Grant that she and I may find mercy
and that we may grow old together."
(**Tobit 8:5-7**)

Your wife will be like a fruitful vine
within your house;
your children will be like olive shoots
around your table.
Thus shall the man be blessed
who fears the LORD.
(**Psalm 128:3-4**)

Beloved, let us love one another, because love is from God; everyone who loves is born of God and knows God. Whoever does not love does not know God, for God is love. (**1 John 4:7-8**)

A Blessed Wife

A wife's charm delights her husband,
and her skill puts flesh on his bones.
A silent wife is a gift from the Lord,
and nothing is so precious as her self-discipline.
A modest wife adds charm to charm,
and no scales can weigh the value of her chastity.

Like the sun rising in the heights of the Lord,
    so is the beauty of a good wife in her
        well-ordered home.
Like the shining lamp on the holy lampstand,
    so is a beautiful face on a stately figure.
Like golden pillars on silver bases,
    so are shapely legs and steadfast feet.
(Sirach 26:13-18)

A capable wife who can find?
    She is far more precious than jewels.
The heart of her husband trusts in her,
    and he will have no lack of gain.
She does him good, and not harm,
    all the days of her life.
She seeks wool and flax,
    and works with willing hands. . . .
She girds herself with strength,
    and makes her arms strong.
She perceives that her merchandise is profitable.
    Her lamp does not go out at night.
She puts her hands to the distaff,
    and her hands hold the spindle.
She opens her hand to the poor,
    and reaches out her hands to the needy.
She is not afraid for her household when it snows,
    for all her household are clothed in crimson. . . .
Strength and dignity are her clothing,

and she laughs at the time to come.
She opens her mouth with wisdom,
    and the teaching of kindness is on her tongue.
She looks well to the ways of her household,
    and does not eat the bread of idleness.
Her children rise up and call her happy;
    her husband too, and he praises her:
"Many women have done excellently,
    but you surpass them all."
Charm is deceitful, and beauty is vain,
    but a woman who fears the LORD is to be praised.
Give her a share in the fruit of her hands,
    and let her works praise her in the city gates.
(Proverbs 31:10-13, 17-21, 25-31)

House and wealth are inherited from parents,
    but a prudent wife is from the LORD.
(Proverbs 19:14)

For Newlyweds

I take pleasure in three things,
    and they are beautiful in the sight of God
        and of mortals:
agreement among brothers and sisters,

friendship among neighbors,
and a wife and a husband who live in harmony.
(Sirach 25:1)

The LORD has done great things for us,
and we rejoiced.
(Psalm 126:3)

For this reason I bow my knees before the Father, from whom every family in heaven and on earth takes its name. I pray that, according to the riches of his glory, he may grant that you may be strengthened in your inner being with power through his Spirit, and that Christ may dwell in your hearts through faith, as you are being rooted and grounded in love. I pray that you may have the power to comprehend, with all the saints, what is the breadth and length and height and depth, and to know the love of Christ that surpasses knowledge, so that you may be filled with all the fullness of God. **(Ephesians 3:14-19)**

And this is my prayer, that your love may overflow more and more with knowledge and full insight to help you to determine what is best, so that in the day of Christ you may be pure and blameless, having produced the harvest of righteousness that comes through Jesus Christ for the glory and praise of God. **(Philippians 1:9-11)**

As God's chosen ones, holy and beloved, clothe yourselves with compassion, kindness, humility, meekness, and patience. Bear with one another and, if anyone has a complaint against another, forgive each other; just as the Lord has forgiven you, so you also must forgive. Above all, clothe yourselves with love, which binds everything together in perfect harmony. And let the peace of Christ rule in your hearts, to which indeed you were called in the one body. (**Colossians 3:12-15**)

The Blessing of Children

Sons are indeed a heritage from the LORD,
    the fruit of the womb a reward.
Like arrows in the hand of a warrior
    are the sons of one's youth.
Happy is the man who has
    his quiver full of them.
He shall not be put to shame
    when he speaks with his enemies in the gate.
(**Psalm 127:3-5**)

May the LORD give you increase,
    both you and your children.
May you be blessed by the LORD,
    who made heaven and earth.
The heavens are the LORD's heavens,

but the earth he has given to human beings. . . .
We will bless the LORD
    from this time on and forevermore.
Praise the LORD!
(Psalm 115:14-16, 18)

And as for me, this is my covenant with them, says the LORD: my spirit that is upon you, and my words that I have put in your mouth, shall not depart out of your mouth, or out of the mouths of your children, or out of the mouths of your children's children, says the LORD, from now on and forever. (Isaiah 59:21)

He who disciplines his son will profit by him,
    and will boast of him among acquaintances.
He who teaches his son will make his enemies envious,
    and will glory in him among his friends.
When the father dies he will not seem to be dead,
    for he has left behind him one like himself,
whom in his life he looked upon with joy
    and at death, without grief.
(Sirach 30:2-5)

Listen to me your father, O children;
    act accordingly, that you may be kept in safety.
For the Lord honors a father above his children,
    and he confirms a mother's right over her children.
Those who honor their father atone for sins,

and those who respect their mother are like
    those who lay up treasure.
Those who honor their father will have
    joy in their own children,
    and when they pray they will be heard.
Those who respect their father will have long life,
    and those who honor their mother obey the Lord;
    they will serve their parents as their masters.
Honor your father by word and deed,
    that his blessing may come upon you.
(Sirach 3:1-8)

"Let the little children come to me; do not stop them; for it is to such as these that the kingdom of God belongs. Truly I tell you, whoever does not receive the kingdom of God as a little child will never enter it." **(Mark 10:14-15)**

PART TWO

SCRIPTURE AND THE COMMUNION OF SAINTS

The communion of saints is the church—those living and those already in heaven with God. Together we are united with Christ as our head. As one body, it's important that we offer up prayers for one another. Our Father must be pleased when he hears the prayers and petitions of his people for their brothers and sisters in Christ. "Christian intercession participates in Christ's, as an expression of the communion of saints" (*Catechism of the Catholic Church*, 2635).

In this section, we have included Scripture passages so that you can pray for the church—that it stay pure and anchored in Christ and his saving work—and for the members of the church, ourselves included, that we will follow Jesus' command to preach to the nations. We have also included a chapter so that you can pray for the dead. It has always been the tradition of the church to honor the memory of the dead, especially for the souls in purgatory, and to offer prayers for them, "so that, thus purified, they may attain the beatific vision of God" (CCC, 1032). Scripture offers us great consolation that not only are our loved ones who have gone before us in the hands of God, but that together we will be raised from the dead and experience bodily resurrection.

The church has always prayed to the saints, who are truly our heroic brothers and sisters in Christ. One chapter honors Mary, the Mother of God, the first of all saints and the Mother of the church. Another chapter is for all the saints, and includes Scripture passages that remind all of us that we are called to be saints. Finally, we have included a chapter on the angels. Although the angels are not part of the communion of saints, they are God's creation and "the whole life of the Church benefits from the mysterious and powerful help of angels" (CCC, 334).

Chapter 8 | *For the Church*

Ascribe to the LORD, O families of the peoples,
    ascribe to the LORD glory and strength.
Ascribe to the LORD the glory due his name;
    bring an offering, and come into his courts.
Worship the LORD in holy splendor;
    tremble before him, all the earth.
Say among the nations, "The LORD is king!
    The world is firmly established;
        it shall never be moved.
    He will judge the peoples with equity."
Let the heavens be glad, and let the earth rejoice;
    let the sea roar, and all that fills it;

let the field exult, and everything in it.
Then shall all the trees of the forest sing for joy
    before the Lord; for he is coming,
    for he is coming to judge the earth.
He will judge the world with righteousness,
    and the peoples with his truth.
(Psalm 96:7-13)

All the nations you have made shall come
    and bow down before you, O Lord,
    and shall glorify your name.
For you are great and do wondrous things;
    you alone are God.
(Psalm 86:9-10)

All the ends of the earth shall remember
    and turn to the Lord;
and all the families of the nations
    shall worship before him.
For dominion belongs to the Lord,
    and he rules over the nations.
To him, indeed, shall all who sleep in the earth
        bow down;
    before him shall bow all who go down to the dust,
    and I shall live for him.
Posterity will serve him;
    future generations will be told about the Lord,
and proclaim his deliverance to a people yet unborn,

saying that he has done it.
(Psalm 22:27-31)

Simon Peter answered, "You are the Messiah, the Son of the living God." And Jesus answered him, "Blessed are you, Simon son of Jonah! For flesh and blood has not revealed this to you, but my Father in heaven. And I tell you, you are Peter, and on this rock I will build my church, and the gates of Hades will not prevail against it. I will give you the keys of the kingdom of heaven, and whatever you bind on earth will be bound in heaven, and whatever you loose on earth will be loosed in heaven."
(Matthew 16:16-19)

The Body Has Many Members

For just as the body is one and has many members, and all the members of the body, though many, are one body, so it is with Christ. For in the one Spirit we were all baptized into one body—Jews or Greeks, slaves or free—and we were all made to drink of one Spirit.

Indeed, the body does not consist of one member but of many. (1 Corinthians 12:12-14)

"You are the salt of the earth; but if salt has lost its taste, how can its saltiness be restored? It is no longer good for anything, but is thrown out and trampled under foot.

"You are the light of the world. A city built on a hill cannot be hid. No one after lighting a lamp puts it under the bushel basket, but on the lampstand, and it gives light to all in the house. In the same way, let your light shine before others, so that they may see your good works and give glory to your Father in heaven." (**Matthew 5:13-16**)

And Jesus came and said to them, "All authority in heaven and on earth has been given to me. Go therefore and make disciples of all nations, baptizing them in the name of the Father and of the Son and of the Holy Spirit, and teaching them to obey everything that I have commanded you. And remember, I am with you always, to the end of the age." (**Matthew 28:18-20**)

Do all things without murmuring and arguing, so that you may be blameless and innocent, children of God without blemish in the midst of a crooked and perverse generation, in which you shine like stars in the world. It is by your holding fast to the word of life that I can boast on the day of Christ that I did not run in vain or labor in vain. (**Philippians 2:14-16**)

So let us not grow weary in doing what is right, for we will reap at harvest-time, if we do not give up. So then, whenever we have an opportunity, let us work for the good of all, and especially for those of the family of faith. (**Galatians 6:9-10**)

Chapter 9 | *For the Dead*

The noble Judas . . . took up a collection, man by man, to the amount of two thousand drachmas of silver, and sent it to Jerusalem to provide for a sin offering. In doing this he acted very well and honorably, taking account of the resurrection. For if he were not expecting that those who had fallen would rise again, it would have been superfluous and foolish to pray for the dead. But if he was looking to the splendid reward that is laid up for those who fall asleep in godliness, it was a holy and pious thought. Therefore he made atonement for the dead, so that they might be delivered from their sin. (**2 Maccabees 12:42-45**)

In the Hands of God

The souls of the righteous are in the hand of God,
and no torment will ever touch them.
In the eyes of the foolish they seemed to have died,
and their departure was thought to be a disaster,
and their going from us to be their destruction;
but they are at peace.
For though in the sight of others they were punished,
their hope is full of immortality.
Having been disciplined a little, they will receive
great good,

because God tested them and found them
>   worthy of himself;
like gold in the furnace he tried them,
and like a sacrificial burnt offering he accepted them.
In the time of their visitation they will shine forth,
and will run like sparks through the stubble.
They will govern nations and rule over peoples,
and the Lord will reign over them forever.
Those who trust in him will understand truth,
and the faithful will abide with him in love,
because grace and mercy are upon his holy ones,
and he watches over his elect.
(**Wisdom 3:1-9**)

"Do not let your hearts be troubled. Believe in God, believe also in me. In my Father's house there are many dwelling places. If it were not so, would I have told you that I go to prepare a place for you? And if I go and prepare a place for you, I will come again and will take you to myself, so that where I am, there you may be also." (**John 14:1-3**)

We do not want you to be uninformed, brothers and sisters, about those who have died, so that you may not grieve as others do who have no hope. For since we believe that Jesus died and rose again, even so, through Jesus, God will bring with him those who have died.
(**1 Thessalonians 4:13-14**)

I heard a voice from heaven saying, "Write this: Blessed are the dead who from now on die in the Lord." "Yes," says the Spirit, "they will rest from their labors, for their deeds follow them." **(Revelation 14:13)**

The Dead Will Be Raised

For I know that my Redeemer lives,
>   and that at the last he will stand upon the earth;
and after my skin has been thus destroyed,
>   then in my flesh I shall see God,
whom I shall see on my side,
>   and my eyes shall behold, and not another.
(Job 19:25-27)

But if Christ is in you, though the body is dead because of sin, the Spirit is life because of righteousness. If the Spirit of him who raised Jesus from the dead dwells in you, he who raised Christ from the dead will give life to your mortal bodies also through his Spirit that dwells in you.
(Romans 8:10-11)

"And as for the resurrection of the dead, have you not read what was said to you by God, 'I am the God of Abraham, the God of Isaac, and the God of Jacob'? He is God not of the dead, but of the living."
(Matthew 22:31-32)

Listen, I will tell you a mystery! We will not all die, but we will all be changed, in a moment, in the twinkling of an eye, at the last trumpet. For the trumpet will sound, and the dead will be raised imperishable, and we will be changed. (**1 Corinthians 15:51-52**)

Blessed and holy are those who share in the first resurrection. Over these the second death has no power, but they will be priests of God and of Christ, and they will reign with him a thousand years. (**Revelation 20:6**)

Chapter 10 | *In Honor of Mary*

I will cause your name to be celebrated
    in all generations;
  therefore the peoples will praise you
    forever and ever.
(**Psalm 45:17**)

A great portent appeared in heaven: a woman clothed with the sun, with the moon under her feet, and on her head a crown of twelve stars. She was pregnant and was crying out in birth pangs, in the agony of giving birth. Then another portent appeared in heaven: a great red dragon, with seven heads and ten horns, and seven diadems on his heads. His tail swept down a third of the stars of heaven and threw them to the earth. Then the dragon stood before the woman who was about to bear a child, so that he might devour her child as soon as it was born. And she gave birth to a son, a male child, who is to rule all the nations with a rod of iron. But her child was snatched away and taken to God and to his throne; and the woman fled into the wilderness, where she has a place prepared by God. (**Revelation 12:1-6**)

Mary's Fiat: Doing God's Will

Mary said, "Here am I, the servant of the Lord; let it be with me according to your word." (**Luke 1:38**)

"Blessed are you among women, and blessed is the fruit of your womb. . . . And blessed is she who believed that there would be a fulfillment of what was spoken to her by the Lord." (**Luke 1:42, 45**)

"My soul magnifies the Lord,
    and my spirit rejoices in God my Savior,
for he has looked with favor on the lowliness
        of his servant.
    Surely, from now on all generations will
        call me blessed;
for the Mighty One has done great things for me,
    and holy is his name.

His mercy is for those who fear him
    from generation to generation.
He has shown strength with his arm;
    he has scattered the proud in the thoughts
        of their hearts.
He has brought down the powerful from their thrones,
    and lifted up the lowly;
he has filled the hungry with good things,
    and sent the rich away empty.
He has helped his servant Israel,
    in remembrance of his mercy,
according to the promise he made to our ancestors,
    to Abraham and to his descendants forever."
(**Luke 1:46-55**)

While they were there, the time came for her to deliver her child. And she gave birth to her firstborn son and wrapped him in bands of cloth, and laid him in a manger, because there was no place for them in the inn. (**Luke 2:6-7**)

All this took place to fulfill what had been spoken by the Lord through the prophet:
    "Look, the virgin shall conceive and bear a son,
        and they shall name him Emmanuel,"
which means, "God is with us." (**Matthew 1:22-23**)

His mother said to the servants, "Do whatever he tells you." (**John 2:5**)

[The shepherds] went with haste and found Mary and Joseph, and the child lying in the manger. When they saw this, they made known what had been told them about this child; and all who heard it were amazed at what the shepherds told them. But Mary treasured all these words and pondered them in her heart. (**Luke 2:16-19**)

Simeon blessed them and said to his mother Mary, "This child is destined for the falling and the rising of many in Israel, and to be a sign that will be opposed so that the inner thoughts of many will be revealed—and a sword will pierce your own soul too." (**Luke 2:34-35**)

Then his mother and his brothers came to him, but they could not reach him because of the crowd. And he was told, "Your mother and your brothers are standing outside, wanting to see you." But he said to them, "My mother and my brothers are those who hear the word of God and do it." (**Luke 8:19-21**)

Chapter 11 | *In Honor of the Saints*

Let all who take refuge in you rejoice;
    let them ever sing for joy.
Spread your protection over them,
    so that those who love your name may
        exult in you.
For you bless the righteous, O LORD;
    you cover them with favor as with a shield.
(Psalm 5:11-12)

As for the holy ones in the land, they are the noble,
    in whom is all my delight.
(Psalm 16:3)

The Saints in Heaven

When he had taken the scroll, the four living creatures and the twenty-four elders fell before the Lamb, each holding a harp and golden bowls full of incense, which are the prayers of the saints. They sing a new song:
    "You are worthy to take the scroll
        and to open its seals,
for you were slaughtered and by your blood
        you ransomed for God
        saints from every tribe and language and people

and nation;
you have made them to be a kingdom and priests
    serving our God,
    and they will reign on earth." (**Revelation 5:8-10**)

I looked, and there was a great multitude that no one could count, from every nation, from all tribes and peoples and languages, standing before the throne and before the Lamb, robed in white, with palm branches in their hands. They cried out in a loud voice, saying,
    "Salvation belongs to our God who is seated on the
        throne, and to the Lamb!" . . .
And all the angels stood around the throne and around the elders and the four living creatures, and they fell on their faces before the throne and worshiped God, singing,
    "Amen! Blessing and glory and wisdom
    and thanksgiving and honor
    and power and might
    be to our God forever and ever! Amen."
Then one of the elders addressed me, saying, "Who are these, robed in white, and where have they come from?" I said to him, "Sir, you are the one that knows." Then he said to me, "These are they who have come out of the great ordeal; they have washed their robes and made them white in the blood of the Lamb." (**Revelation 7:9-14**)

"Hallelujah!
For the Lord our God

the Almighty reigns.
Let us rejoice and exult
    and give him the glory,
for the marriage of the Lamb has come,
    and his bride has made herself ready;
to her it has been granted to be clothed
    with fine linen, bright and pure"—
for the fine linen is the righteous deeds of the saints.
(**Revelation 19:6-8**)

Called to Be Saints

To all God's beloved, . . . who are called to be saints: Grace
to you and peace from God our Father and the Lord Jesus
Christ. (**Romans 1:7**)

Since we are surrounded by so great a cloud of witnesses,
let us also lay aside every weight and the sin that clings so
closely, and let us run with perseverance the race that is set
before us, looking to Jesus the pioneer and perfecter of our
faith. (**Hebrews 12:1-2**)

So then you are no longer strangers and aliens, but you are
citizens with the saints and also members of the household
of God, built upon the foundation of the apostles and
prophets, with Christ Jesus himself as the cornerstone.
In him the whole structure is joined together and grows

into a holy temple in the Lord; in whom you also are built together spiritually into a dwelling place for God. (**Ephesians 2:19-22**)

Here is a call for the endurance of the saints, those who keep the commandments of God and hold fast to the faith of Jesus. (**Revelation 14:12**)

May the Lord make you increase and abound in love for one another and for all. . . . And may he so strengthen your hearts in holiness that you may be blameless before our God and Father at the coming of our Lord Jesus with all his saints. (**1 Thessalonians 3:12-13**)

Now concerning love of the brothers and sisters, you do not need to have anyone write to you, for you yourselves have been taught by God to love one another; and indeed you do love all the brothers and sisters. . . . But we urge you, beloved, to do so more and more. (**1 Thessalonians 4:9-10**)

Chapter 12 | *In Honor of the Angels*

Praise the LORD!
Praise the LORD from the heavens;
  praise him in the heights!
Praise him, all his angels;

praise him, all his host! . . .
Let them praise the name of the LORD,
    for he commanded and they were created.
He established them forever and ever.
(Psalm 148:1-2, 5-6a)

Blessed are you in the temple of your holy glory,
    and to be extolled and highly glorified forever.
Blessed are you who look into the depths from
      your throne on the cherubim,
    and to be praised and highly exalted forever.
Blessed are you on the throne of your kingdom,
    and to be extolled and highly exalted forever.
Blessed are you in the firmament of heaven,
    and to be sung and glorified forever.
Bless the Lord, all you works of the Lord;
    sing praise to him and highly exalt him forever.
Bless the Lord, you heavens;
    sing praise to him and highly exalt him forever.
Bless the Lord, you angels of the Lord;
    sing praise to him and highly exalt him forever.
(Daniel 3:53-59)

Blessed be God,
    and blessed be his great name,
    and blessed be all his holy angels.

May his holy name be blessed
throughout all the ages.
(**Tobit 11:14**)

Because you have made the LORD your refuge,
the Most High your dwelling place,
no evil shall befall you,
no scourge come near your tent.
For he will command his angels concerning you
to guard you in all your ways.
On their hands they will bear you up,
so that you will not dash your foot against a stone.
(**Psalm 91:9-12**)

Then I looked, and I heard the voice of many angels surrounding the throne and the living creatures and the elders; they numbered myriads of myriads and thousands of thousands, singing with full voice,
"Worthy is the Lamb that was slaughtered
to receive power and wealth and wisdom and might
and honor and glory and blessing!"
(**Revelation 5:11-12**)

God's Heavenly Messengers

"I am Raphael, one of the seven angels who stand ready and enter before the glory of the Lord. . . .

"Do not be afraid; peace be with you. Bless God forevermore. As for me, when I was with you, I was not acting on my own will, but by the will of God. Bless him each and every day; sing his praises." (**Tobit 12:15, 17-18**)

"I am Gabriel. I stand in the presence of God, and I have been sent to speak to you and to bring you this good news." . . . The angel said to her, "Do not be afraid, Mary, for you have found favor with God." (**Luke 1:19, 30**)

And suddenly there was with the angel a multitude of the heavenly host, praising God and saying,
    "Glory to God in the highest heaven,
    and on earth peace among those whom he favors!"
(**Luke 2:13-14**)

"Take care that you do not despise one of these little ones; for, I tell you, in heaven their angels continually see the face of my Father in heaven." (**Matthew 18:10**)

And the angels waited on him. (**Mark 1:13**)

PART THREE

IN TIMES OF NEED

God wants us to turn to him with our every need. He is our Father, and he cares for us. As Jesus reassured us, he has already counted every hair on our head (Luke 12:7). However, when we find ourselves in difficult or trying situations, we can be tempted to doubt that awesome truth. In those times, Scripture can be a tremendous blessing. So many passages can help us to increase our trust in God and to believe in faith that he will answer our prayers and meet our needs.

In this section, you will find Scripture passages that speak to a wide variety of situations. Perhaps you are in financial need or struggling with a difficult relationship. Perhaps you are suffering from anxiety, loneliness, or depression. Perhaps you need guidance. Scripture can exhort us in all these circumstances to depend on our loving Father and to trust in his love. If you know someone who is in need, you may want to encourage them with one of these passages. As we pray these Scripture verses, we internalize the truths they contain. Then not only will the Lord lift us up, but he will use us to be an inspiration to others.

Chapter 13 | *For God's Provision*

The eyes of all look to you,
  and you give them their food in due season.
You open your hand,
  satisfying the desire of every living thing.
(Psalm 145:15-16)

"Therefore I tell you, do not worry about your life, what you will eat or what you will drink, or about your body, what you will wear. Is not life more than food, and the body more than clothing? Look at the birds of the air; they neither sow nor reap nor gather into barns, and yet your heavenly Father feeds them. Are you not of more value than they? And can any of you by worrying add a single hour to your span of life? And why do you worry about clothing? Consider the lilies of the field, how they grow; they neither toil nor spin, yet I tell you, even Solomon in all his glory was not clothed like one of these. But if God so clothes the grass of the field, which is alive today and tomorrow is thrown into the oven, will he not much more clothe you—you of little faith? Therefore do not worry, saying, 'What will we eat?' or 'What will we drink?' or 'What will we wear?' For it is the Gentiles who strive for all these things; and indeed your heavenly Father knows that you need all these things. But strive first for the kingdom of God and his righteousness, and all these things will be given to you as well.

"So do not worry about tomorrow, for tomorrow will bring worries of its own. Today's trouble is enough for today." (Matthew 6:25-34)

Claiming God's Promises

When the poor and needy seek water,
    and there is none,
    and their tongue is parched with thirst,
I the LORD will answer them,
    I the God of Israel will not forsake them.
I will open rivers on the bare heights,
    and fountains in the midst of the valleys;
I will make the wilderness a pool of water,
    and the dry land springs of water.
I will put in the wilderness the cedar,
    the acacia, the myrtle, and the olive;
I will set in the desert the cypress,
    the plane and the pine together,
so that all may see and know,
    all may consider and understand,
that the hand of the LORD has done this,
    the Holy One of Israel has created it.
(Isaiah 41:17-20)

I will make them and the region around my hill a blessing; and I will send down the showers in their season; they shall be showers of blessing. The trees of the field shall yield their fruit, and the earth shall yield its increase. They shall be secure on their soil; and they shall know that I am the LORD, when I break the bars of their yoke, and save them from the hands of those who enslaved them. . . . They shall live in safety, and no one shall make them afraid. I will provide for them a splendid vegetation so that they shall no more be consumed with hunger in the land, and no longer suffer the insults of the nations. They shall know that I, the LORD their God am with them, and that they, the house of Israel, are my people, says the Lord GOD. You are my sheep, the sheep of my pasture and I am your God, says the Lord GOD. (**Ezekiel 34:26-31**)

"Ask, and it will be given you; search, and you will find; knock, and the door will be opened for you. For everyone who asks receives, and everyone who searches finds, and for everyone who knocks, the door will be opened. Is there anyone among you who, if your child asks for bread, will give a stone? Or if the child asks for a fish, will give a snake? If you then, who are evil, know how to give good gifts to your children, how much more will your Father in heaven give good things to those who ask him!"
(**Matthew 7:7-11**)

The prayer of the righteous is powerful and effective. Elijah was a human being like us, and he prayed fervently that it might not rain, and for three years and six months it did not rain on the earth. Then he prayed again, and the heaven gave rain and the earth yielded its harvest. (James 5:16-18)

Dependence on God

Hear the voice of my supplication,
    as I cry to you for help,
as I lift up my hands
    toward your most holy sanctuary.
(Psalm 28:2)

Trust in the LORD, and do good;
    so you will live in the land, and enjoy security.
Take delight in the LORD,
    and he will give you the desires of your heart.
Commit your way to the LORD;
    trust in him, and he will act.
He will make your vindication shine like the light,
    and the justice of your cause like the noonday.
Be still before the LORD, and wait patiently for him;
    do not fret over those who prosper in their way,
    over those who carry out evil devices.
Refrain from anger, and forsake wrath.

Do not fret—it leads only to evil.
For the wicked shall be cut off,
>but those who wait for the LORD shall
>>inherit the land.

(Psalm 37:3-9)

Though the fig tree does not blossom,
>and no fruit is on the vines;
though the produce of the olive fails,
>and the fields yield no food;
though the flock is cut off from the fold,
>and there is no herd in the stalls,
yet I will rejoice in the LORD;
>I will exult in the God of my salvation.
GOD, the Lord, is my strength;
>he makes my feet like the feet of a deer,
>and makes me tread upon the heights.

(Habakkuk 3:17-19)

For God alone my soul waits in silence,
>for my hope is from him.
He alone is my rock and my salvation,
>my fortress; I shall not be shaken.
On God rests my deliverance and my honor;
>my mighty rock, my refuge is in God.
Trust in him at all times, O people;

pour out your heart before him;
    God is a refuge for us.
(Psalm 62:5-8)

Gratitude for God's Blessings

O give thanks to the LORD, for he is good;
    for his steadfast love endures forever.
Let the redeemed of the LORD say so,
    those he redeemed from trouble. . . .
Hungry and thirsty,
    their soul fainted within them.
Then they cried to the LORD in their trouble,
    and he delivered them from their distress. . . .
Let them thank the LORD for his steadfast love,
    for his wonderful works to humankind.
For he satisfies the thirsty,
    and the hungry he fills with good things.
(Psalm 107:1-2, 5-6, 8-9)

O give thanks to the LORD, call on his name,
    make known his deeds among the peoples.
Sing to him, sing praises to him,
    tell of all his wonderful works.
Glory in his holy name;
    let the hearts of those who seek the LORD rejoice.
Seek the LORD and his strength,

seek his presence continually.
Remember the wonderful works he has done,
    his miracles, and the judgments he uttered.
(**1 Chronicles 16:8-12**)

Give thanks to the Lord, for he is good,
    for his mercy endures forever.
All who worship the Lord, bless the God of gods,
    sing praise to him and give thanks to him,
        for his mercy endures forever.
(**Daniel 3:89-90**)

Rejoice always, pray without ceasing, give thanks in all circumstances; for this is the will of God in Christ Jesus for you. (**1 Thessalonians 5:16-18**)

Chapter 14 | *For Needs of the Heart*

"Come to me, all you that are weary and are carrying heavy burdens, and I will give you rest. Take my yoke upon you, and learn from me; for I am gentle and humble in heart, and you will find rest for your souls. For my yoke is easy, and my burden is light." (**Matthew 11:28-30**)

Freedom from Fear

Who is like me? Let them proclaim it,
   let them declare and set it forth before me.
Who has announced from of old the things to come?
   Let them tell us what is yet to be.
Do not fear, or be afraid;
   have I not told you from of old and declared it?
   You are my witnesses!
Is there any god besides me?
   There is no other rock; I know not one.
(Isaiah 44:7-8)

A windstorm arose on the sea, so great that the boat was being swamped by the waves; but he was asleep. And they went and woke him up, saying, "Lord, save us! We are perishing!" And he said to them, "Why are you afraid, you of little faith?" Then he got up and rebuked the winds and the sea; and there was a dead calm. (Matthew 8:24-26)

"Take heart, it is I; do not be afraid." (Mark 6:50)

✓ Do not fear, for I have redeemed you;
   I have called you by name, you are mine.
When you pass through the waters, I will be with you;
   and through the rivers, they shall not
      overwhelm you;
when you walk through fire you shall not be burned,

and the flame shall not consume you.
For I am the LORD your God,
    the Holy One of Israel, your Savior. . . .
Because you are precious in my sight,
    and honored, and I love you,
I give people in return for you,
    nations in exchange for your life.
Do not fear, for I am with you;
    I will bring your offspring from the east,
    and from the west I will gather you;
I will say to the north, "Give them up,"
    and to the south, "Do not withhold;
bring my sons from far away
    and my daughters from the end of the earth—
everyone who is called by my name,
    whom I created for my glory,
    whom I formed and made."
(Isaiah 43:1-3a, 4-7)

The LORD answer you in the day of trouble!
    The name of the God of Jacob protect you!
May he send you help from the sanctuary,
    and give you support from Zion.
May he remember all your offerings,
    and regard with favor your burnt sacrifices.
May he grant you your heart's desire,
    and fulfill all your plans.
May we shout for joy over your victory,

and in the name of our God set up our banners.
May the LORD fulfill all your petitions.
Now I know that the LORD will help his anointed;
    he will answer him from his holy heaven
    with mighty victories by his right hand.
Some take pride in chariots, and some in horses,
    but our pride is in the name of the LORD our God.
(Psalm 20:1-7)

Freedom from Worry and Anxiety

Our soul waits for the LORD;
    he is our help and shield.
Our heart is glad in him,
    because we trust in his holy name.
Let your steadfast love, O LORD, be upon us,
    even as we hope in you.
(Psalm 33:20-22)

Let all who are faithful
    offer prayer to you;
at a time of distress, the rush of mighty waters
    shall not reach them.
You are a hiding place for me;
    you preserve me from trouble;
    you surround me with glad cries of deliverance.
(Psalm 32:6-7)

Cast your burden on the LORD,
> and he will sustain you;
he will never permit
> the righteous to be moved.
(Psalm 55:22)

Do not worry about anything, but in everything by prayer and supplication with thanksgiving let your requests be made known to God. And the peace of God, which surpasses all understanding, will guard your hearts and your minds in Christ Jesus. **(Philippians 4:6-7)**

"Peace I leave with you; my peace I give to you. I do not give to you as the world gives. Do not let your hearts be troubled, and do not let them be afraid." **(John 14:27)**

Humble yourselves therefore under the mighty hand of God, so that he may exalt you in due time. Cast all your anxiety on him, because he cares for you. **(1 Peter 5:6-7)**

Therefore, since we are justified by faith, we have peace with God through our Lord Jesus Christ. **(Romans 5:1)**

Freedom from Depression

Sing praises to the LORD, O you his faithful ones,
> and give thanks to his holy name.

For his anger is but for a moment;
    his favor is for a lifetime.
Weeping may linger for the night,
    but joy comes with the morning. . . .
You have turned my mourning into dancing;
    you have taken off my sackcloth
    and clothed me with joy,
so that my soul may praise you and not be silent.
    O LORD my God, I will give thanks to you forever.
(Psalm 30:4-5, 11-12)

Do not give yourself over to sorrow,
    and do not distress yourself deliberately.
A joyful heart is life itself,
    and rejoicing lengthens one's life span.
Indulge yourself and take comfort,
    and remove sorrow far from you,
for sorrow has destroyed many,
    and no advantage ever comes from it.
Jealousy and anger shorten life,
    and anxiety brings on premature old age.
Those who are cheerful and merry at table
    will benefit from their food.
(Sirach 30:21-25)

You show me the path of life.
In your presence there is fullness of joy;
in your right hand are pleasures forevermore.
(Psalm 16:11)

May those who sow in tears
reap with shouts of joy.
Those who go out weeping,
bearing the seed for sowing,
shall come home with shouts of joy,
carrying their sheaves.
(Psalm 126:5-6)

Praise the LORD!
How good it is to sing praises to our God;
for he is gracious, and a song of praise is fitting. . . .
He heals the brokenhearted,
and binds up their wounds.
(Psalm 147:1, 3)

May the God of hope fill you with all joy and peace in believing, so that you may abound in hope by the power of the Holy Spirit. (Romans 15:13)

"So you have pain now; but I will see you again, and your hearts will rejoice, and no one will take your joy from you." (John 16:22)

Freedom from Loneliness

O LORD, you have searched me and known me.
You know when I sit down and when I rise up;
    you discern my thoughts from far away.
You search out my path and my lying down,
    and are acquainted with all my ways.
Even before a word is on my tongue,
    O LORD, you know it completely.
You hem me in, behind and before,
    and lay your hand upon me.
Such knowledge is too wonderful for me;
    it is so high that I cannot attain it.
Where can I go from your spirit?
    Or where can I flee from your presence?
If I ascend to heaven, you are there;
    if I make my bed in Sheol, you are there.
If I take the wings of the morning
    and settle at the farthest limits of the sea,
even there your hand shall lead me,
    and your right hand shall hold me fast.
If I say, "Surely the darkness shall cover me,
    and the light around me become night,"
even the darkness is not dark to you;
    the night is as bright as the day,
    for darkness is as light to you.
(Psalm 139:1-12)

Do not forsake me, O Lord;
O my God, do not be far from me;
make haste to help me,
O Lord, my salvation.
(**Psalm 38:21-22**)

"I will not leave you orphaned; I am coming to you. In a little while the world will no longer see me, but you will see me; because I live, you also will live. On that day you will know that I am in my Father, and you in me, and I in you." (**John 14:18-20**)

"Remember, I am with you always, to the end of the age." (**Matthew 28:20**)

"For where two or three are gathered in my name, I am there among them." (**Matthew 18:20**)

For Help in Relationships

How very good and pleasant it is
when kindred live together in unity!
It is like the precious oil on the head,
running down upon the beard,
on the beard of Aaron,
running down over the collar of his robes.
It is like the dew of Hermon,

which falls on the mountains of Zion.
For there the LORD ordained his blessing,
life forevermore.
(Psalm 133)

Then Peter came and said to him, "Lord, if another member of the church sins against me, how often should I forgive? As many as seven times?" Jesus said to him, "Not seven times, but, I tell you, seventy-seven times."
(Matthew 18:21-22)

Putting away falsehood, let all of us speak the truth to our neighbors, for we are members of one another. Be angry but do not sin; do not let the sun go down on your anger, and do not make room for the devil. . . . Let no evil talk come out of your mouths, but only what is useful for building up, as there is need, so that your words may give grace to those who hear. And do not grieve the Holy Spirit of God, with which you were marked with a seal for the day of redemption. Put away from you all bitterness and wrath and anger and wrangling and slander, together with all malice, and be kind to one another, tenderhearted, forgiving one another, as God in Christ has forgiven you. Therefore be imitators of God, as beloved children, and live in love, as Christ loved us and gave himself up for us, a fragrant offering and sacrifice to God.
(Ephesians 4:25-27, 29–5:2)

✓ Let love be genuine; hate what is evil, hold fast to what is good; love one another with mutual affection; outdo one another in showing honor. Do not lag in zeal, be ardent in spirit, serve the Lord. Rejoice in hope, be patient in suffering, persevere in prayer. Contribute to the needs of the saints; extend hospitality to strangers.

Bless those who persecute you; bless and do not curse them. Rejoice with those who rejoice, weep with those who weep. Live in harmony with one another; do not be haughty, but associate with the lowly; do not claim to be wiser than you are. Do not repay anyone evil for evil, but take thought for what is noble in the sight of all. If it is possible, so far as it depends on you, live peaceably with all. (**Romans 12:9-18**)

Love is patient; love is kind; love is not envious or boastful or arrogant or rude. It does not insist on its own way; it is not irritable or resentful; it does not rejoice in wrongdoing, but rejoices in the truth. It bears all things, believes all things, hopes all things, endures all things.

Love never ends. . . . Faith, hope, and love abide, these three; and the greatest of these is love.
(**1 Corinthians 13:4-8, 13**)

The fruit of the Spirit is love, joy, peace, patience, kindness, generosity, faithfulness, gentleness, and self-control. (**Galatians 5:22-23**)

"I give you a new commandment, that you love one another. Just as I have loved you, you also should love one another. By this everyone will know that you are my disciples, if you have love for one another." (**John 13:34-35**)

"Whenever you stand praying, forgive, if you have anything against anyone; so that your Father in heaven may also forgive you your trespasses." (**Mark 11:25**)

Seeking Guidance

With you is wisdom, she who knows your works
and was present when you made the world;
she understands what is pleasing in your sight
and what is right according to your commandments.
Send her forth from the holy heavens,
and from the throne of your glory send her,
that she may labor at my side,
and that I may learn what is pleasing to you.
For she knows and understands all things,
and she will guide me wisely in my actions
and guard me with her glory. . . .
For who can learn the counsel of God?
Or who can discern what the Lord wills?
For the reasoning of mortals is worthless,
and our designs are likely to fail;
for a perishable body weighs down the soul,

and this earthy tent burdens the thoughtful mind.
We can hardly guess at what is on earth,
and what is at hand we find with labor;
but who has traced out what is in the heavens?
Who has learned your counsel,
unless you have given wisdom
and sent your holy spirit from on high?
And thus the paths of those on earth were set right,
and people were taught what pleases you,
and were saved by wisdom.
(**Wisdom 9:9-11, 13-18**)

Make me to know your ways, O LORD;
    teach me your paths.
Lead me in your truth, and teach me,
    for you are the God of my salvation;
    for you I wait all day long.
(**Psalm 25:4-5**)

Teach me, O LORD, the way of your statutes,
    and I will observe it to the end.
Give me understanding, that I may keep your law
    and observe it with my whole heart.
Lead me in the path of your commandments,
    for I delight in it.
Turn my heart to your decrees,
    and not to selfish gain.
Turn my eyes from looking at vanities;

give me life in your ways.
Confirm to your servant your promise,
    which is for those who fear you.
Turn away the disgrace that I dread,
    for your ordinances are good.
See, I have longed for your precepts;
    in your righteousness give me life.
(Psalm 119:33-40)

For surely I know the plans I have for you, says the LORD, plans for your welfare and not for harm, to give you a future with hope. Then when you call upon me and come and pray to me, I will hear you. When you search for me, you will find me; if you seek me with all your heart. (Jeremiah 29:11-13)

I will lead the blind
    by a road they do not know,
by paths they have not known
    I will guide them.
I will turn the darkness before them into light,
    the rough places into level ground.
These are the things I will do,
    and I will not forsake them.
    (Isaiah 42:16)

"My sheep hear my voice. I know them, and they follow me." (John 10:27)

Overcoming Temptation

Trouble and anguish have come upon me,
    but your commandments are my delight.
Your decrees are righteous forever;
    give me understanding that I may live.
With my whole heart I cry; answer me, O LORD.
    I will keep your statutes.
I cry to you; save me,
    that I may observe your decrees.
(Psalm 119:143-146)

Be merciful to me, O God, be merciful to me,
    for in you my soul takes refuge;
in the shadow of your wings I will take refuge,
    until the destroying storms pass by.
I cry to God Most High,
    to God who fulfills his purpose for me.
He will send from heaven and save me,
    he will put to shame those who trample on me.
God will send forth his steadfast love and
      his faithfulness.
(Psalm 57:1-3)

Blessed is anyone who endures temptation. Such a one has stood the test and will receive the crown of life that the Lord has promised to those who love him. **(James 1:12)**

No testing has overtaken you that is not common to everyone. God is faithful, and he will not let you be tested beyond your strength, but with the testing he will also provide the way out so that you may be able to endure it. (**1 Corinthians 10:13**)

Therefore he had to become like his brothers and sisters in every respect, so that he might be a merciful and faithful high priest in the service of God, to make a sacrifice of atonement for the sins of the people. Because he himself was tested by what he suffered, he is able to help those who are being tested. (**Hebrews 2:17-18**)

Discipline yourselves, keep alert. Like a roaring lion your adversary the devil prowls around, looking for someone to devour. Resist him, steadfast in your faith, for you know that your brothers and sisters in all the world are undergoing the same kinds of suffering. And after you have suffered for a little while, the God of all grace, who has called you to his eternal glory in Christ, will himself restore, support, strengthen, and establish you. (**1 Peter 5:8-10**)

For Protection from Evil

You who live in the shelter of the Most High,
  who abide in the shadow of the Almighty,
will say to the LORD, "My refuge and my fortress;

my God, in whom I trust."
For he will deliver you from the snare of the fowler
 and from the deadly pestilence;
he will cover you with his pinions,
 and under his wings you will find refuge;
 his faithfulness is a shield and buckler.
You will not fear the terror of the night,
 or the arrow that flies by day,
or the pestilence that stalks in darkness,
 or the destruction that wastes at noonday.
A thousand may fall at your side,
 ten thousand at your right hand,
 but it will not come near you.
You will only look with your eyes
 and see the punishment of the wicked.
Because you have made the LORD your refuge,
 the Most High your dwelling place,
no evil shall befall you,
 no scourge come near your tent.
For he will command his angels concerning you
 to guard you in all your ways.
On their hands they will bear you up,
 so that you will not dash your foot against a stone.
You will tread on the lion and the adder,
 the young lion and the serpent you will
 trample under foot.
Those who love me, I will deliver;
 I will protect those who know my name.

When they call to me, I will answer them;
    I will be with them in trouble,
    I will rescue them and honor them.
With long life I will satisfy them,
    and show them my salvation.
(Psalm 91)

The LORD gives wisdom;
    from his mouth come knowledge and
        understanding;
he stores up sound wisdom for the upright;
    he is a shield to those who walk blamelessly,
guarding the paths of justice
    and preserving the way of his faithful ones.
Then you will understand righteousness and justice
    and equity, every good path;
for wisdom will come into your heart,
    and knowledge will be pleasant to your soul;
prudence will watch over you,
    and understanding will guard you.
It will save you from the way of evil,
    from those who speak perversely,
who forsake the paths of uprightness
    to walk in the ways of darkness,
who rejoice in doing evil
    and delight in the perverseness of evil;

those whose paths are crooked,
    and who are devious in their ways.
(**Proverbs 2:6-15**)

I lift up my eyes to the hills—
    from where will my help come?
My help comes from the LORD,
    who made heaven and earth.
He will not let your foot be moved;
    he who keeps you will not slumber.
He who keeps Israel
    will neither slumber nor sleep.
The LORD is your keeper;
    the LORD is your shade at your right hand.
The sun shall not strike you by day,
    nor the moon by night.
The LORD will keep you from all evil;
    he will keep your life.
The LORD will keep
    your going out and your coming in
    from this time on and forevermore.
(**Psalm 121**)

Hear my cry, O God;
    listen to my prayer.
From the end of the earth I call to you,
    when my heart is faint.
Lead me to the rock

that is higher than I;
for you are my refuge,
   a strong tower against the enemy.
Let me abide in your tent forever,
   find refuge under the shelter of your wings.
(Psalm 61:1-4)

Be strong in the Lord and in the strength of his power. Put on the whole armor of God, so that you may be able to stand against the wiles of the devil. For our struggle is not against enemies of blood and flesh, but against the rulers, against the authorities, against the cosmic powers of this present darkness, against the spiritual forces of evil in the heavenly places. Therefore take up the whole armor of God, so that you may be able to withstand on that evil day, and having done everything, to stand firm. Stand therefore, and fasten the belt of truth around your waist, and put on the breastplate of righteousness. As shoes for your feet put on whatever will make you ready to proclaim the gospel of peace. With all of these, take the shield of faith, with which you will be able to quench all the flaming arrows of the evil one. Take the helmet of salvation, and the sword of the Spirit, which is the word of God. **(Ephesians 6:10-17)**

PART FOUR

FOR ALL TIMES AND SEASONS

"In Christianity time has a fundamental importance," the late Pope John Paul II wrote in his 1994 apostolic letter *Tertio Millennio Adveniente*. "Within the dimension of time the world was created; within it the history of salvation unfolds, finding its culmination in the 'fullness of time' of the Incarnation, and its goal in the glorious return of the Son of God at the end of time." And from this relationship of God with time, "there arises the duty to sanctify time" (10).

How can we sanctify our time? The passages and prayers in this section will help you to turn to the Lord at all times of the day. Whether we are waking up in the morning to greet a new day, saying a blessing before our meals, or going about our daily work, we can sanctify time by directing our hearts and minds to the Lord of all time. In this way we can follow the commandment of Jesus to "Abide in me" (John 15:4).

We can enter more fully into the celebration of the liturgical seasons by praying the passages provided here for each season, for Holy Week, and for major feasts. As we do so, we can see the breadth and expanse of God's plan of salvation, from the beginning when he called a people to himself to the fulfillment of time in his Son, Jesus. Scripture foretold the great work God would do in Jesus. Let us rejoice with the whole church: Christ has died, Christ is risen, Christ will come again!

Chapter 15 | *Throughout the Day*

Rejoice always, pray without ceasing, give thanks in all circumstances; for this is the will of God in Christ Jesus for you. (**1 Thessalonians 5:16-18**)

> It is good to give thanks to the LORD,
>   to sing praises to your name, O Most High;
> to declare your steadfast love in the morning,
>   and your faithfulness by night,
> to the music of the lute and the harp,
>   to the melody of the lyre.
> For you, O LORD, have made me glad by your work;
>   at the works of your hands I sing for joy.
> How great are your works, O LORD!
>   Your thoughts are very deep! . . .
>   You, O LORD, are on high forever.
> (**Psalm 92:1-5, 8**)

The LORD bless you and keep you;
the LORD make his face to shine upon you,
    and be gracious to you;
the LORD lift up his countenance upon you,
    and give you peace.
(**Numbers 6:24-26**)

In the Morning

LORD, in the morning you hear my voice;
    in the morning I plead my case to you, and watch.
(**Psalm 5:3**)

O LORD, be gracious to us; we wait for you.
    Be our arm every morning,
    our salvation in the time of trouble.
(**Isaiah 33:2**)

This is the day that the LORD has made;
    let us rejoice and be glad in it.
Save us, we beseech you, O LORD!
    O LORD, we beseech you, give us success!
(**Psalm 118:24-25**)

My heart is steadfast, O God,
    my heart is steadfast.
I will sing and make melody.

Awake, my soul!
Awake, O harp and lyre!
  I will awake the dawn.
I will give thanks to you, O Lord, among the peoples;
  I will sing praises to you among the nations.
For your steadfast love is as high as the heavens;
  your faithfulness extends to the clouds.
Be exalted, O God, above the heavens.
  Let your glory be over all the earth.
(Psalm 57:7-11)

I rise before dawn and cry for help;
  I put my hope in your words.
My eyes are awake before each watch of the night,
  that I may meditate on your promise.
In your steadfast love hear my voice;
  O LORD, in your justice preserve my life.
(Psalm 119:147-49)

The steadfast love of the LORD never ceases,
  his mercies never come to an end;
they are new every morning;
  great is your faithfulness.
"The LORD is my portion," says my soul,
  "therefore I will hope in him."
The LORD is good to those who wait for him,

to the soul that seeks him.
It is good that one should wait quietly
    for the salvation of the LORD.
(**Lamentations 3:22-26**)

For the Workplace

And whatever you do, in word or deed, do everything in the name of the Lord Jesus, giving thanks to God the Father through him. (**Colossians 3:17**)

Unless the LORD builds the house,
    those who build it labor in vain.
Unless the LORD guards the city,
    the guard keeps watch in vain.
It is in vain that you rise up early
    and go late to rest,
eating the bread of anxious toil;
    for he gives sleep to his beloved.
(**Psalm 127:1-2**)

Let your work be manifest to your servants,
    and your glorious power to their children.
Let the favor of the Lord our God be upon us,
    and prosper for us the work of our hands—
    O prosper the work of our hands!
(**Psalm 90:16-17**)

Remember the sabbath day, and keep it holy. Six days you shall labor and do all your work. But the seventh day is a sabbath to the LORD your God. (**Exodus 20:8-10**)

Therefore, my beloved, be steadfast, immovable, always excelling in the work of the Lord, because you know that in the Lord your labor is not in vain.
(**1 Corinthians 15:58**)

> O LORD, my heart is not lifted up,
>   my eyes are not raised too high;
> I do not occupy myself with things
>   too great and too marvelous for me.
> But I have calmed and quieted my soul,
>   like a weaned child with its mother;
>   my soul is like the weaned child that is with me.
> O Israel, hope in the LORD
>   from this time on and forevermore.
> (**Psalm 131**)

Before Meals

> Bless the LORD, O my soul.
>   O LORD my God, you are very great. . . .
> You cause the grass to grow for the cattle,
>   and plants for people to use,
> to bring forth food from the earth,

and wine to gladden the human heart,
oil to make the face shine
and bread to strengthen the human heart. . . .
O LORD how manifold are your works!
In wisdom you have made them all;
the earth is full of your creatures. . . .
These all look to you
to give them their food in due season;
when you give to them, they gather it up;
when you open your hand, they are filled with
good things. . . .
Bless the LORD, O my soul.
Praise the LORD!
(Psalm 104:1, 14-15, 24, 27-28, 35)

O give thanks to the LORD, for he is good,
for his steadfast love endures forever.
O give thanks to the God of gods,
for his steadfast love endures forever.
O give thanks to the Lord of lords,
for his steadfast love endures forever;
who alone does great wonders,
for his steadfast love endures forever;
who by understanding made the heavens,
for his steadfast love endures forever;
who spread out the earth on the waters,
for his steadfast love endures forever;
who made the great lights,

for his steadfast love endures forever;
the sun to rule over the day,
     for his steadfast love endures forever;
the moon and stars to rule over the night,
     for his steadfast love endures forever; . . .
It is he who . . . gives food to all flesh,
     for his steadfast love endures forever.
O give thanks to the God of heaven,
     for his steadfast love endures forever.
(Psalm 136:1-9, 23, 25-26)

Let them thank the LORD for his steadfast love,
     for his wonderful works to humankind.
For he satisfies the thirsty,
     and the hungry he fills with good things.
(Psalm 107:8-9)

Happy are those whose help is the God of Jacob,
     whose hope is in the LORD their God,
who made heaven and earth,
     the sea, and all that is in them;
who keeps faith forever;
     who executes justice for the oppressed;
     who gives food to the hungry.
The LORD sets the prisoners free;
     the LORD opens the eyes of the blind.
The LORD lifts up those who are bowed down;
     the LORD loves the righteous. . . .

The LORD will reign forever,
    your God, O Zion, for all generations.
Praise the LORD!
(Psalm 146:5-8, 10)

In the Evening

Answer me when I call, O God of my right!
    You gave me room when I was in distress.
    Be gracious to me, and hear my prayer. . . .
But know that the LORD has set apart the faithful
        for himself;
    the LORD hears when I call to him.
When you are disturbed, do not sin;
    ponder it on your beds, and be silent.
Offer right sacrifices,
    and put your trust in the LORD.
There are many who say, "O that we might see
        some good!
    Let the light of your face shine on us, O LORD!"
You have put gladness in my heart
    more than when their grain and wine abound.
I will both lie down and sleep in peace;
    for you alone, O LORD, make me lie down in safety.
(Psalm 4:1, 3-8)

Because your steadfast love is better than life,
    my lips will praise you.
So I will bless you as long as I live;
    I will lift up my hands and call on your name.
My soul is satisfied as with a rich feast,
    and my mouth praises you with joyful lips
when I think of you on my bed,
    and meditate on you in the watches of the night;
for you have been my help,
    and in the shadow of your wings I sing for joy.
My soul clings to you;
    your right hand upholds me.
(Psalm 63:3-8)

In the path of your judgments,
    O LORD, we wait for you;
your name and your renown
    are the soul's desire.
My soul yearns for you in the night,
    my spirit within me earnestly seeks you.
For when your judgments are in the earth,
    the inhabitants of the world learn righteousness.
(Isaiah 26:8-9)

I remember your name in the night, O LORD,
    and keep your law.

This blessing has fallen to me,
   for I have kept your precepts.
(Psalm 119:55-56)

You, O LORD, are a shield around me,
   my glory, and the one who lifts up my head.
I cry aloud to the LORD,
   and he answers me from his holy hill.
I lie down and sleep;
   I wake again, for the LORD sustains me.
(Psalm 3:3-5)

Chapter 16 | *Advent*

See, I am sending my messenger to prepare the way before me, and the Lord whom you seek will suddenly come to his temple. The messenger of the covenant in whom you delight—indeed, he is coming, says the LORD of hosts. But who can endure the day of his coming, and who can stand when he appears? For he is like a refiner's fire and like full-ers' soap; he will sit as a refiner and purifier of silver, and he will purify the descendants of Levi and refine them like gold and silver, until they present offerings to the LORD in righteousness. (**Malachi 3:1-3**)

Prepare the Way

Then his father Zechariah was filled with the Holy Spirit and spoke this prophecy:
"Blessed be the Lord God of Israel,
    for he has looked favorably on his people and
        redeemed them.
He has raised up a mighty savior for us
    in the house of his servant David,
as he spoke through the mouth of his holy prophets
        from of old,
    that we would be saved from our enemies and from
        the hand of all who hate us.
Thus he has shown the mercy promised to
        our ancestors,
    and has remembered his holy covenant,
the oath that he swore to our ancestor Abraham,
    to grant us that we, being rescued from the hands
        of our enemies,
might serve him without fear, in holiness
        and righteousness
    before him all our days.
And you, child, will be called the prophet of
        the Most High;
    for you will go before the Lord to prepare his ways,
to give knowledge of salvation to his people
    by the forgiveness of their sins.
By the tender mercy of our God,

the dawn from on high will break upon us,
to give light to those who sit in darkness
and in the shadow of death,
to guide our feet into the way of peace."
(Luke 1:67-79)

It is now the moment for you to wake from sleep. For salvation is nearer to us now than when we became believers; the night is far gone, the day is near. Let us then lay aside the works of darkness and put on the armor of light; let us live honorably as in the day, not in reveling and drunkenness, not in debauchery and licentiousness, not in quarreling and jealousy. Instead, put on the Lord Jesus Christ, and make no provision for the flesh, to gratify its desires.
(Romans 13:11-14)

"Come, let us go up to the mountain of the Lord,
to the house of the God of Jacob;
that he may teach us his ways
and that we may walk in his paths."
(Isaiah 2:3)

Comfort, O comfort my people,
says your God.
Speak tenderly to Jerusalem,
and cry to her
that she has served her term,
that her penalty is paid,

that she has received from the LORD's hand
  double for all her sins.
A voice cries out:
"In the wilderness prepare the way of the LORD,
  make straight in the desert a highway for our God.
Every valley shall be lifted up,
  and every mountain and hill be made low;
the uneven ground shall become level,
  and the rough places a plain.
Then the glory of the LORD shall be revealed,
  and all people shall see it together,
  for the mouth of the LORD has spoken."
(Isaiah 40:1-5)

The Savior Comes

But as for you, have no fear, my servant Jacob,
  says the LORD,
  and do not be dismayed, O Israel;
for I am going to save you from far away,
  and your offspring from the land of their captivity.
Jacob shall return and have quiet and ease,
  and no one shall make him afraid.
For I am with you, says the LORD, to save you.
(Jeremiah 30:10-11)

The Lord himself will give you a sign. Look, the young woman is with child and shall bear a son, and shall name him Immanuel. (Isaiah 7:14)

I am the LORD, and there is no other;
    besides me there is no god.
    I arm you, though you do not know me,
so that they may know, from the rising of the sun
    and from the west, that there is no one besides me;
    I am the LORD, and there is no other.
I form light and create darkness,
    I make weal and create woe;
    I the LORD do all these things.
Shower, O heavens, from above,
    and let the skies rain down righteousness;
let the earth open, that salvation may spring up,
    and let it cause righteousness to sprout up also;
    I the LORD have created it.
(Isaiah 45:5-8)

Remember me, O LORD, when you show favor
        to your people;
    help me when you deliver them;
that I may see the prosperity of your chosen ones,
    that I may rejoice in the gladness of your nation,
    that I may glory in your heritage.
(Psalm 106:4-5)

I will sprinkle clean water upon you, and you shall be clean from all your uncleannesses, and from all your idols I will cleanse you. A new heart I will give you, and a new spirit I will put within you; and I will remove from your body the heart of stone and give you a heart of flesh. I will put my spirit within you, and make you follow my statutes and be careful to observe my ordinances. Then you shall live in the land that I gave to your ancestors; and you shall be my people, and I will be your God. I will save you from all your uncleannesses. (**Ezekiel 36:25-29**)

> I call upon you, for you will answer me, O God;
> > incline your ear to me, hear my words.
> Wondrously show your steadfast love,
> > O savior of those who seek refuge
> > from their adversaries at your right hand.
> (**Psalm 17:6-7**)

He Comes Again!

> Let your steadfast love come to me, O LORD,
> > your salvation according to your promise.
> (**Psalm 119:41**)

Our citizenship is in heaven, and it is from there that we are expecting a Savior, the Lord Jesus Christ. He will transform the body of our humiliation that it may be conformed to the body of his glory, by the power that also enables him to make all things subject to himself.

Therefore, my brothers and sisters, whom I love and long for, my joy and crown, stand firm in the Lord in this way, my beloved. (**Philippians 3:20–4:1**)

With the Lord one day is like a thousand years, and a thousand years are like one day. The Lord is not slow about his promise, as some think of slowness, but is patient with you, not wanting any to perish, but all to come to repentance. But the day of the Lord will come like a thief, and then the heavens will pass away with a loud noise, and the elements will be dissolved with fire, and the earth and everything that is done on it will be disclosed.

Since all these things are to be dissolved in this way, what sort of persons ought you to be in leading lives of holiness and godliness, waiting for and hastening the coming of the day of God, because of which the heavens will be set ablaze and dissolved, and the elements will melt with fire? But, in accordance with his promise, we wait for new heavens and a new earth, where righteousness is at home.

Therefore, beloved, while you are waiting for these things, strive to be found by him at peace, without spot or blemish; and regard the patience of our Lord as salvation. . . .

Beware that you are not carried away with the error of the lawless and lose your own stability. But grow in the grace and knowledge of our Lord and Savior Jesus Christ.

To him be the glory both now and to the day of eternity. Amen. (**2 Peter 3:8-15, 17-18**)

Do not pronounce judgment before the time, before the Lord comes, who will bring to light the things now hidden in darkness and will disclose the purposes of the heart. Then each one will receive commendation from God. (**1 Corinthians 4:5**)

Be patient, therefore, beloved, until the coming of the Lord. The farmer waits for the precious crop from the earth, being patient with it until it receives the early and the late rains. You also must be patient. Strengthen your hearts, for the coming of the Lord is near. Beloved, do not grumble against one another, so that you may not be judged. See, the Judge is standing at the doors! As an example of suffering and patience, beloved, take the prophets who spoke in the name of the Lord. Indeed we call blessed those who showed endurance. You have heard of the endurance of Job, and you have seen the purpose of the Lord, how the Lord is compassionate and merciful. (**James 5:7-11**)

"The sign of the Son of Man will appear in heaven, and then all the tribes of the earth will mourn, and they will see 'the Son of Man coming on the clouds of heaven' with power and great glory. And he will send out his angels with a loud trumpet call, and they will gather his elect from the four winds, from one end of heaven to the other.

"From the fig tree learn its lesson: as soon as its branch becomes tender and puts forth its leaves, you know that summer is near. So also, when you see all these things, you know that he is near, at the very gates. Truly I tell you, this generation will not pass away until all these things have taken place. Heaven and earth will pass away, but my words will not pass away." (**Matthew 24:30-35**)

Amen. Come, Lord Jesus! (**Revelation 22:20**)

Chapter 17 | *Christmas*

In the beginning was the Word, and the Word was with God, and the Word was God. He was in the beginning with God. All things came into being through him, and without him not one thing came into being. What has come into being in him was life, and the life was the light of all people. The light shines in the darkness, and the darkness did not overcome it. . . .

He was in the world, and the world came into being through him; yet the world did not know him. He came to what was his own, and his own people did not accept him. But to all who received him, who believed in his name, he gave power to become children of God, who were born, not of blood or of the will of the flesh or of the will of man, but of God.

And the Word became flesh and lived among us, and we have seen his glory, the glory as of a father's only son, full of grace and truth. (**John 1:1-5, 10-14**)

A Child Is Born

A child has been born for us,
    a son given to us;
authority rests upon his shoulders;
    and he is named
Wonderful Counselor, Mighty God,
    Everlasting Father, Prince of Peace.
His authority shall grow continually,
    and there shall be endless peace
for the throne of David and his kingdom.
    He will establish and uphold it
with justice and with righteousness
    from this time onward and forevermore.
The zeal of the Lord of hosts will do this.
(**Isaiah 9:6-7**)

Joseph also went from the town of Nazareth in Galilee to Judea, to the city of David called Bethlehem, because he was descended from the house and family of David. He went to be registered with Mary, to whom he was engaged and who was expecting a child. While they were there, the time came for her to deliver her child. And she gave birth to her firstborn son and wrapped him in bands of cloth, and laid him in a manger, because there was no place for them in the inn.

In that region there were shepherds living in the fields, keeping watch over their flock by night. Then an angel of the Lord stood before them, and the glory of the Lord shone around them, and they were terrified. But the angel said to them, "Do not be afraid; for see—I am bringing you good news of great joy for all the people: to you is born this day in the city of David a Savior, who is the Messiah, the Lord. This will be a sign for you: you will find a child wrapped in bands of cloth and lying in a manger." And suddenly there was with the angel a multitude of the heavenly host, praising God and saying,

"Glory to God in the highest heaven,
   and on earth peace among those whom he favors!"

When the angels had left them and gone into heaven, the shepherds said to one another, "Let us go now to Bethlehem and see this thing that has taken place, which the Lord has made known to us." So they went with haste and found Mary and Joseph, and the child lying in the manger. When they saw this, they made known what had been told them about this child; and all who heard it were amazed at what the shepherds told them. But Mary treasured all these words and pondered them in her heart. The shepherds returned, glorifying and praising God for all they had heard and seen, as it had been told them.
(Luke 2:4-20)

Good Tidings

Get you up to a high mountain,
    O Zion, herald of good tidings;
lift up your voice with strength,
    O Jerusalem, herald of good tidings,
    lift it up, do not fear;
say to the cities of Judah,
    "Here is your God!"
See, the Lord GOD comes with might,
    and his arm rules for him;
his reward is with him,
    and his recompense before him.
He will feed his flock like a shepherd;
    he will gather the lambs in his arms,
and carry them in his bosom,
    and gently lead the mother sheep.
(Isaiah 40:9-11)

Make a joyful noise to God, all the earth;
    sing the glory of his name;
    give to him glorious praise.
Say to God, "How awesome are your deeds! . . .
All the earth worships you;
    they sing praises to you,
    sing praises to your name."

Come and see what God has done:
    he is awesome in his deeds among mortals.
(Psalm 66:1-5)

O give thanks to the LORD, call on his name,
    make known his deeds among the peoples.
Sing to him, sing praises to him;
    tell of all his wonderful works.
Glory in his holy name;
    let the hearts of those who seek the LORD rejoice.
Seek the LORD and his strength;
    seek his presence continually.
Remember the wonderful works he has done,
    his miracles, and the judgments he has uttered. . . .
He is the LORD our God;
    his judgments are in all the earth.
He is mindful of his covenant forever,
    of the word that he commanded,
        for a thousand generations.
(Psalm 105:1-5, 7-8)

Open to me the gates of righteousness,
    that I may enter through them
    and give thanks to the LORD.
This is the gate of the LORD;
    the righteous shall enter through it.
I thank you that you have answered me
    and have become my salvation.

The stone that the builders rejected
      has become the chief cornerstone.
This is the LORD's doing;
      it is marvelous in our eyes.
This is the day that the LORD has made;
      let us rejoice and be glad in it.
Save us, we beseech you, O LORD!
      O LORD, we beseech you, give us success!
Blessed is the one who comes in the name of the LORD.
      We bless you from the house of the LORD.
The LORD is God,
      and he has given us light.
Bind the festal procession with branches,
      up to the horns of the altar.
You are my God, and I will give thanks to you;
      you are my God, I will extol you.
O give thanks to the LORD, for he is good,
      for his steadfast love endures forever.
(Psalm 118:19-29)

Chapter 18 | *Epiphany*

Arise, shine; for your light has come,
      and the glory of the LORD has risen upon you.
For darkness shall cover the earth,
      and thick darkness the peoples;
but the LORD will arise upon you,

and his glory will appear over you.
Nations shall come to your light,
    and kings to the brightness of your dawn.
Lift up your eyes and look around;
    they all gather together, they come to you;
your sons shall come from far away,
    and your daughters shall be carried
        on their nurses' arms.
Then you shall see and be radiant;
    your heart shall thrill and rejoice,
because the abundance of the sea shall be
        brought to you,
    the wealth of the nations shall come to you.
A multitude of camels shall cover you,
    the young camels of Midian and Ephah;
    all those from Sheba shall come.
They shall bring gold and frankincense,
    and shall proclaim the praise of the LORD.
(Isaiah 60:1-6)

Wise men from the East came to Jerusalem, asking, "Where is the child who has been born king of the Jews? For we observed his star at its rising, and have come to pay him homage." . . . It has been written by the prophet:
    'And you, Bethlehem, in the land of Judah,
        are by no means least among the rulers of Judah;
    for from you shall come a ruler
        who is to shepherd my people Israel.'" . . .

They set out; and there, ahead of them, went the star that they had seen at its rising, until it stopped over the place where the child was. When they saw that the star had stopped, they were overwhelmed with joy. On entering the house, they saw the child with Mary his mother; and they knelt down and paid him homage. Then, opening their treasure chests, they offered him gifts of gold, frankincense, and myrrh. (**Matthew 2:1-2, 5-6, 9-11**)

A Light to the Nations

A bright light will shine to all the ends of the earth;
   many nations will come to you from far away,
the inhabitants of the remotest parts of the earth
      to your holy name,
   bearing gifts in their hands for the King of heaven.
Generation after generation will give joyful praise
      in you. (**Tobit 13:11**)

The people who walked in darkness
   have seen a great light;
those who lived in a land of deep darkness—
   on them light has shined.
You have multiplied the nation,
   you have increased its joy;
they rejoice before you
   as with joy at the harvest,

as people exult when dividing plunder.
For the yoke of their burden,
    and the bar across their shoulders,
    the rod of their oppressor,
    you have broken as on the day of Midian.
(Isaiah 9:2-4)

I will extol you, my God and King,
    and bless your name forever and ever.
Every day I will bless you,
    and praise your name forever and ever.
Great is the LORD, and greatly to be praised;
    his greatness is unsearchable.
One generation shall laud your works to another,
    and shall declare your mighty acts.
On the glorious splendor of your majesty,
    and on your wondrous works, I will meditate.
The might of your awesome deeds
      shall be proclaimed,
    and I will declare your greatness.
They shall celebrate the fame of your
      abundant goodness,
    and shall sing aloud of your righteousness.
The LORD is gracious and merciful,
    slow to anger and abounding in steadfast love.
The LORD is good to all,
    and his compassion is over all that he has made.
All your works shall give thanks to you, O LORD,

and all your faithful shall bless you.
They shall speak of the glory of your kingdom,
    and tell of your power,
to make known to all people your mighty deeds,
    and the glorious splendor of your kingdom.
Your kingdom is an everlasting kingdom,
    and your dominion endures throughout
        all generations.
(Psalm 145:1-13)

Save us, O LORD our God,
    and gather us from among the nations,
that we may give thanks to your holy name
    and glory in your praise.
Blessed be the LORD, the God of Israel,
    from everlasting to everlasting.
And let all the people say, "Amen."
    Praise the LORD!
(Psalm 106:47-48)

Sing to God, O kingdoms of the earth;
    sing praises to the Lord,
O rider in the heavens, the ancient heavens;
    listen, he sends out his voice, his mighty voice.
Ascribe power to God,
    whose majesty is over Israel;
    and whose power is in the skies.
Awesome is God in his sanctuary,

the God of Israel;
        he gives power and strength to his people.
Blessed be God!
(**Psalm 68:32-35**)

Chapter 19 | *Lent*

Return to me, and I will return to you, says the LORD of hosts. (**Malachi 3:7**)

O give thanks to the LORD, . . .
who struck Egypt through their firstborn,
        for his steadfast love endures forever;
and brought Israel out from among them,
        for his steadfast love endures forever;
with a strong hand and an outstretched arm,
        for his steadfast love endures forever;
who divided the Red Sea in two,
        for his steadfast love endures forever;
and made Israel pass through the midst of it,
        for his steadfast love endures forever;
but overthrew Pharaoh and his army in the Red Sea,
        for his steadfast love endures forever;
who led his people through the wilderness,
        for his steadfast love endures forever;
who struck down great kings,
        for his steadfast love endures forever; . . .

and gave their land as a heritage,
for his steadfast love endures forever;
a heritage to his servant Israel,
for his steadfast love endures forever.
It is he who remembered us in our low estate,
for his steadfast love endures forever;
and rescued us from our foes,
for his steadfast love endures forever;
who gives food to all flesh,
for his steadfast love endures forever.
O give thanks to the God of heaven,
for his steadfast love endures forever.
(Psalm 136:1, 10-17, 21-26)

A Time to Repent

*[For additional prayers of repentance, see Chapter 4 on
the Sacrament of Reconciliation.]*

Even now, says the LORD,
return to me with all your heart,
with fasting, with weeping, and with mourning;
rend your hearts and not your clothing.
Return to the LORD, your God,
for he is gracious and merciful,
slow to anger, and abounding in steadfast love,
and relents from punishing.

Who knows whether he will not turn and relent,
    and leave a blessing behind him,
a grain offering and a drink offering
    for the LORD, your God?
Blow the trumpet in Zion;
    sanctify a fast;
call a solemn assembly;
    gather the people.
Sanctify the congregation;
    assemble the aged;
gather the children,
    even infants at the breast.
Let the bridegroom leave his room,
    and the bride her canopy.
Between the vestibule and the altar
    let the priests, the ministers of the LORD, weep.
Let them say, "Spare your people, O LORD,
    and do not make your heritage a mockery,
    a byword among the nations.
Why should it be said among the peoples,
    'Where is their God?'"
(Joel 2:12-17)

Blessed be God who lives forever,
    because his kingdom lasts throughout all ages.
For he afflicts, and he shows mercy; . . .
    he brings up from the great abyss,
    and there is nothing that can escape his hand. . . .

Exalt him in the presence of every living being,
    because he is our Lord and he is our God;
    he is our Father and he is God forever.
He will afflict you for your iniquities,
    but he will again show mercy on all of you. . . .
If you turn to him with all your heart and with
      all your soul,
    to do what is true before him,
then he will turn to you
    and will no longer hide his face from you.
So now see what he has done for you;
    acknowledge him at the top of your voice.
Bless the Lord of righteousness,
    and exalt the King of the ages. . . .
"Turn back, you sinners, and do what is right
      before him;
    perhaps he may look with favor upon you
      and show you mercy."
As for me, I exalt my God,
    and my soul rejoices in the King of heaven.
Let all people speak of his majesty,
    and acknowledge him. . . .
    He afflicted you for the deeds of your hands,
    but will again have mercy on the children
      of the righteous.
Acknowledge the Lord, for he is good,
    and bless the King of the ages,
    so that his tent may be rebuilt in you in joy. . . .

My soul blesses the Lord, the great King! . . .
"Blessed be the God of Israel!"
  and the blessed will bless the holy name
    forever and ever.
(Tobit 13:1-2, 4-8, 9-10, 15, 17)

We entreat you on behalf of Christ, be reconciled to God.
For our sake he made him to be sin who knew no sin, so
that in him we might become the righteousness of God.
  As we work together with him, we urge you also not to
accept the grace of God in vain. For he says,
  "At an acceptable time I have listened to you,
    and on a day of salvation I have helped you."
See, now is the acceptable time; see, now is the day of sal-
vation! (2 Corinthians 5:20–6:2)

See, I have set before you today life and prosperity, death
and adversity. If you obey the commandments of the LORD
your God that I am commanding you today, by loving the
LORD your God, walking in his ways, and observing his
commandments, decrees, and ordinances, then you shall
live and become numerous, and the LORD your God will
bless you in the land that you are entering to possess. But
if your heart turns away and you do not hear, but are led
astray to bow down to other gods and serve them, I declare
to you today that you shall perish; you shall not live long in
the land that you are crossing the Jordan to enter and possess. I call heaven and earth to witness against you today

that I have set before you life and death, blessings and curses. Choose life so that you and your descendants may live, loving the LORD your God, obeying him, and holding fast to him; for that means life to you and length of days, so that you may live in the land that the LORD swore to give to your ancestors, to Abraham, to Isaac, and to Jacob. (Deuteronomy 30:15-20)

"If any want to become my followers, let them deny themselves and take up their cross daily and follow me. For those who want to save their life will lose it, and those who lose their life for my sake will save it. What does it profit them if they gain the whole world, but lose or forfeit themselves?" (Luke 9:23-25)

"Those who are well have no need of a physician, but those who are sick; I have come to call not the righteous but sinners to repentance." (Luke 5:31-32)

Fasting and Almsgiving

Is not this the fast that I choose:
 to loose the bonds of injustice,
 to undo the thongs of the yoke,
to let the oppressed go free,
 and to break every yoke?
Is it not to share your bread with the hungry,

and bring the homeless poor into your house;
when you see the naked, to cover them,
    and not to hide yourself from your own kin?
Then your light shall break forth like the dawn,
    and your healing shall spring up quickly;
your vindicator shall go before you,
    the glory of the LORD shall be your rear guard.
Then you shall call, and the LORD will answer;
    you shall cry for help, and he will say, Here I am.
If you remove the yoke from among you,
    the pointing of the finger, the speaking of evil,
if you offer your food to the hungry
    and satisfy the needs of the afflicted,
then your light shall rise in the darkness
    and your gloom be like the noonday.
The LORD will guide you continually,
    and satisfy your needs in parched places,
    and make your bones strong;
and you shall be like a watered garden,
    like a spring of water,
    whose waters never fail.
Your ancient ruins shall be rebuilt;
    you shall raise up the foundations
        of many generations;
you shall be called the repairer of the breach,
    the restorer of streets to live in.
If you refrain from trampling the sabbath,
    from pursuing your own interests on my holy day;

if you call the sabbath a delight
    and the holy day of the LORD honorable;
if you honor it, not going your own ways,
    serving your own interests, or pursuing
        your own affairs;
then you shall take delight in the LORD,
    and I will make you ride upon the heights
        of the earth;
I will feed you with the heritage of
    your ancestor Jacob,
    for the mouth of the LORD has spoken.
(Isaiah 58:6-14)

Prayer with fasting is good, but better than both is almsgiving with righteousness. A little with righteousness is better than wealth with wrongdoing. It is better to give alms than to lay up gold. For almsgiving saves from death and purges away every sin. Those who give alms will enjoy a full life, but those who commit sin and do wrong are their own worst enemies. **(Tobit 12:8-10)**

"Beware of practicing your piety before others in order to be seen by them; for then you have no reward from your Father in heaven.

"So whenever you give alms, do not sound a trumpet before you, as the hypocrites do in the synagogues and in the streets, so that they may be praised by others. Truly I tell you, they have received their reward. But when you give alms, do not let your left hand know what your right hand is doing, so that your alms may be done in secret; and your Father who sees in secret will reward you. . . .

"And whenever you fast, do not look dismal, like the hypocrites, for they disfigure their faces so as to show others that they are fasting. Truly I tell you, they have received their reward. But when you fast, put oil on your head and wash your face, so that your fasting may be seen not by others but by your Father who is in secret; and your Father who sees in secret will reward you."
(Matthew 6:1-4, 16-18)

Chapter 20 | *Holy Week*

Rejoice greatly, O daughter Zion!
    Shout aloud, O daughter Jerusalem!
Lo, your king comes to you;
    triumphant and victorious is he,
humble and riding on a donkey,
    on a colt, the foal of a donkey.
(Zechariah 9:9)

They brought the donkey and the colt, and put their cloaks on them, and he sat on them. A very large crowd spread their cloaks on the road, and others cut branches from the trees and spread them on the road. The crowds that went ahead of him and that followed were shouting,

"Hosanna to the Son of David!
    Blessed is the one who comes in the name
        of the Lord!
Hosanna in the highest heaven!" **(Matthew 21:7-9)**

[Jesus] said to them, "I have eagerly desired to eat this Passover with you before I suffer; for I tell you, I will not eat it until it is fulfilled in the kingdom of God." **(Luke 22:15-16)**

He has appeared once for all at the end of the age to remove sin by the sacrifice of himself. **(Hebrews 9:26)**

Christ Jesus, . . .
    though he was in the form of God,
        did not regard equality with God
        as something to be exploited,
    but emptied himself,
        taking the form of a slave,
        being born in human likeness.
    And being found in human form,
        he humbled himself
        and became obedient to the point of death—
        even death on a cross.
    Therefore God also highly exalted him
        and gave him the name
        that is above every name,
    so that at the name of Jesus

every knee should bend,
in heaven and on earth and under the earth,
and every tongue should confess
that Jesus Christ is Lord,
to the glory of God the Father.
(**Philippians 2:5-11**)

Looking to Jesus the pioneer and perfecter of our faith, who for the sake of the joy that was set before him endured the cross, disregarding its shame, and has taken his seat at the right hand of the throne of God.

Consider him who endured such hostility against himself from sinners, so that you may not grow weary or lose heart. In your struggle against sin you have not yet resisted to the point of shedding your blood. (**Hebrews 12:2-4**)

The Suffering Servant

Who has believed what we have heard?
And to whom has the arm of the LORD
been revealed?
For he grew up before him like a young plant,
and like a root out of dry ground;
he had no form or majesty that we should look
at him,
nothing in his appearance that we should
desire him.

He was despised and rejected by others;
    a man of suffering and acquainted with infirmity;
and as one from whom others hide their faces
    he was despised, and we held him of no account.
Surely he has borne our infirmities
    and carried our diseases;
yet we accounted him stricken,
    struck down by God, and afflicted.
But he was wounded for our transgressions,
    crushed for our iniquities;
upon him was the punishment that made us whole,
    and by his bruises we are healed.
All we like sheep have gone astray;
    we have all turned to our own way,
and the LORD has laid on him
    the iniquity of us all.
He was oppressed, and he was afflicted,
    yet he did not open his mouth;
like a lamb that is led to the slaughter,
    and like a sheep that before its shearers is silent,
    so he did not open his mouth.
By a perversion of justice he was taken away.
    Who could have imagined his future?
For he was cut off from the land of the living,
    stricken for the transgression of my people.
They made his grave with the wicked
    and his tomb with the rich,
although he had done no violence,

and there was no deceit in his mouth.
Yet it was the will of the LORD to crush him with pain.
When you make his life an offering for sin,
    he shall see his offspring, and shall prolong
        his days;
through him the will of the LORD shall prosper.
    Out of his anguish he shall see light;
he shall find satisfaction through his knowledge.
    The righteous one, my servant, shall make
        many righteous,
    and he shall bear their iniquities.
Therefore I will allot him a portion with the great,
    and he shall divide the spoil with the strong;
because he poured out himself to death,
    and was numbered with the transgressors;
yet he bore the sin of many,
    and made intercession for the transgressors.
(Isaiah 53)

I will pour out a spirit of compassion and supplication on the house of David and the inhabitants of Jerusalem, so that, when they look on the one whom they have pierced, they shall mourn for him, as one mourns for an only child, and weep bitterly over him, as one weeps over a firstborn. (**Zechariah 12:10**)

Christ also suffered for you, leaving you an example, so that you should follow in his steps.

"He committed no sin,
    and no deceit was found in his mouth."
When he was abused, he did not return abuse; when he suffered, he did not threaten; but he entrusted himself to the one who judges justly. He himself bore our sins in his body on the cross, so that, free from sins, we might live for righteousness; by his wounds you have been healed. For you were going astray like sheep, but now you have returned to the shepherd and guardian of your souls.
(1 Peter 2:21-25)

My God, my God, why have you forsaken me?
    Why are you so far from helping me,
        from the words of my groaning?
O my God, I cry by day, but you do not answer;
    and by night, but find no rest. . . .
But I am a worm, and not human;
    scorned by others, and despised by the people.
All who see me mock at me;
    they make mouths at me, they shake their heads;
"Commit your cause to the LORD; let him deliver—
    let him rescue the one in whom he delights!"
Yet it was you who took me from the womb;
    you kept me safe on my mother's breast.
On you I was cast from my birth,
    and since my mother bore me
        you have been my God.
Do not be far from me,

for trouble is near
and there is no one to help. . . .
I am poured out like water,
and all my bones are out of joint;
my heart is like wax;
it is melted within my breast;
my mouth is dried up like a potsherd,
and my tongue sticks to my jaws;
you lay me in the dust of death.
For dogs are all around me;
a company of evildoers encircles me.
My hands and feet have shriveled;
I can count all my bones.
They stare and gloat over me;
they divide my clothes among themselves,
and for my clothing they cast lots.
But you, O LORD, do not be far away!
O my help, come quickly to my aid!
Deliver my soul from the sword,
my life from the power of the dog!
Save me from the mouth of the lion!
From the horns of the wild oxen you have rescued me.
I will tell of your name to my brothers and sisters;
in the midst of the congregation
I will praise you. . . .
For he did not despise or abhor
the affliction of the afflicted;
he did not hide his face from me;

but heard when I cried to him. . . .
Posterity will serve him;
    future generations will be told about the Lord,
and proclaim his deliverance to a people yet unborn,
    saying that he has done it.
(Psalm 22:1-2, 6-11, 14-22, 24, 30-31)

Jesus the Messiah

There they crucified him, and with him two others, one on either side, with Jesus between them. Pilate also had an inscription written and put on the cross. It read, "Jesus of Nazareth, the King of the Jews." Many of the Jews read this inscription, because the place where Jesus was crucified was near the city; and it was written in Hebrew, in Latin, and in Greek. Then the chief priests of the Jews said to Pilate, "Do not write, 'The King of the Jews,' but, 'This man said, I am King of the Jews.'" Pilate answered, "What I have written I have written." **(John 19:18-22)**

"Truly this man was God's Son!" **(Matthew 27:54)**

He is able for all time to save those who approach God through him, since he always lives to make intercession for them.

For it was fitting that we should have such a high priest, holy, blameless, undefiled, separated from sinners, and exalted above the heavens. Unlike the other high priests, he has no need to offer sacrifices day after day, first for his own sins, and then for those of the people; this he did once for all when he offered himself. (**Hebrews 7:25-27**)

Since, therefore, the children share flesh and blood, he himself likewise shared the same things, so that through death he might destroy the one who has the power of death, that is, the devil, and free those who all their lives were held in slavery by the fear of death. For it is clear that he did not come to help angels, but the descendants of Abraham. Therefore he had to become like his brothers and sisters in every respect, so that he might be a merciful and faithful high priest in the service of God, to make a sacrifice of atonement for the sins of the people. Because he himself was tested by what he suffered, he is able to help those who are being tested. (**Hebrews 2:14-18**)

"I am the good shepherd. I know my own and my own know me, just as the Father knows me and I know the Father. And I lay down my life for the sheep. I have other sheep that do not belong to this fold. I must bring them also, and they will listen to my voice. So there will be one flock, one shepherd. For this reason the Father loves me, because I lay down my life in order to take it up again. No one takes it from me, but I lay it down of my own accord. I have power to lay it down, and I have power to take it

up again. I have received this command from my Father."
(**John 10:14-18**)

"My kingdom is not from this world. If my kingdom were
from this world, my followers would be fighting to keep
me from being handed over to the Jews. But as it is, my
kingdom is not from here. . . . For this I was born, and for
this I came into the world, to testify to the truth. Everyone
who belongs to the truth listens to my voice."
(**John 18:36, 37**)

To him who loves us and freed us from our sins by his
blood, and made us to be a kingdom, priests serving his
God and Father, to him be glory and dominion forever and
ever. Amen. (**Revelation 1:5-6**)

The Triumph of the Cross

"No one has ascended into heaven except the one who
descended from heaven, the Son of Man. And just as
Moses lifted up the serpent in the wilderness, so must the
Son of Man be lifted up, that whoever believes in him may
have eternal life." (**John 3:13-15**)

"When the Son of Man comes in his glory, and all the
angels with him, then he will sit on the throne of his glory.
All the nations will be gathered before him, and he will

separate people one from another as a shepherd separates the sheep from the goats, and he will put the sheep at his right hand and the goats at the left." (**Matthew 25:31-33**)

And when you were dead in trespasses and the uncircumcision of your flesh, God made you alive together with him, when he forgave us all our trespasses, erasing the record that stood against us with its legal demands. He set this aside, nailing it to the cross. He disarmed the rulers and authorities and made a public example of them, triumphing over them in it. (**Colossians 2:13-15**)

> "The kingdom of the world has become the kingdom
>   of our Lord
>   and of his Messiah,
> and he will reign forever and ever. . . .
> We give you thanks, Lord God Almighty,
>   who are and who were,
> for you have taken your great power
>   and begun to reign."
> (**Revelation 11:15, 17**)

Blessed be the Lord God of Israel,
    for he has looked favorably on his people and
        redeemed them.
He has raised up a mighty savior for us
    in the house of his servant David,
as he spoke through the mouth of his holy prophets

from of old,
    that we would be saved from our enemies and
        from the hand of all who hate us.
Thus he has shown the mercy promised to
        our ancestors,
    and has remembered his holy covenant,
the oath that he swore to our ancestor Abraham,
    to grant us that we, being rescued from the hands
        of our enemies,
might serve him without fear, in holiness
        and righteousness
    before him all our days. . . .
By the tender mercy of our God,
    the dawn from on high will break upon us,
to give light to those who sit in darkness and
        in the shadow of death,
    to guide our feet into the way of peace.
(Luke 1:68-75, 78-79)

May I never boast of anything except the cross of our Lord
Jesus Christ, by which the world has been crucified to me,
and I to the world. **(Galatians 6:14)**

"Worthy is the Lamb that was slaughtered
to receive power and wealth and wisdom and might
and honor and glory and blessing! . . .
To the one seated on the throne and to the Lamb

be blessing and honor and glory and might
forever and ever!"
(**Revelation 5:12, 13**)

Chapter 21 | *Easter*

After the sabbath, as the first day of the week was dawning, Mary Magdalene and the other Mary went to see the tomb. And suddenly there was a great earthquake; for an angel of the Lord, descending from heaven, came and rolled back the stone and sat on it. His appearance was like lightning, and his clothing white as snow. For fear of him the guards shook and became like dead men. But the angel said to the women, "Do not be afraid; I know that you are looking for Jesus who was crucified. He is not here; for he has been raised, as he said. Come, see the place where he lay. Then go quickly and tell his disciples, 'He has been raised from the dead, and indeed he is going ahead of you to Galilee; there you will see him.' This is my message for you." So they left the tomb quickly with fear and great joy, and ran to tell his disciples. Suddenly Jesus met them and said, "Greetings!" And they came to him, took hold of his feet, and worshiped him. Then Jesus said to them, "Do not be afraid; go and tell my brothers to go to Galilee; there they will see me." (**Matthew 28:1-10**)

"My Lord and my God!" (**John 20:28**)

Jesus' Victory

Some sat in darkness and in gloom,
　　prisoners in misery and in irons,
for they had rebelled against the words of God,
　　and spurned the counsel of the Most High.
Their hearts were bowed down with hard labor;
　　they fell down, with no one to help.
Then they cried to the LORD in their trouble,
　　and he saved them from their distress;
he brought them out of darkness and gloom,
　　and broke their bonds asunder.
Let them thank the LORD for his steadfast love,
　　for his wonderful works to humankind.
For he shatters the doors of bronze,
　　and cuts in two the bars of iron.
(Psalm 107:10-16)

Your right hand, O LORD, glorious in power—
　　your right hand, O LORD, shattered the enemy.
In the greatness of your majesty you overthrew
　　　　your adversaries;
　　you sent out your fury, it consumed them
　　　　like stubble.
(Exodus 15:6-7)

In him we have redemption through his blood, the forgiveness of our trespasses, according to the riches of his grace

that he lavished on us. With all wisdom and insight he has made known to us the mystery of his will, according to his good pleasure that he set forth in Christ, as a plan for the fullness of time, to gather up all things in him, things in heaven and things on earth. (**Ephesians 1:7-10**)

"Death has been swallowed up in victory."
"Where, O death, is your victory?
   Where, O death, is your sting?"
The sting of death is sin, and the power of sin is the law. But thanks be to God, who gives us the victory through our Lord Jesus Christ. (**1 Corinthians 15:54-57**)

O give thanks to the LORD, for he is good;
   his steadfast love endures forever! . . .
The LORD is my strength and my might;
   he has become my salvation.
There are glad songs of victory in the tents
      of the righteous:
"The right hand of the LORD does valiantly;
   the right hand of the LORD is exalted;
   the right hand of the LORD does valiantly."
I shall not die, but I shall live,
   and recount the deeds of the LORD. . . .
Open to me the gates of righteousness,
   that I may enter through them
   and give thanks to the LORD.
This is the gate of the LORD;

the righteous shall enter through it.
I thank you that you have answered me
    and have become my salvation.
The stone that the builders rejected
    has become the chief cornerstone.
This is the LORD's doing;
    it is marvelous in our eyes.
This is the day that the LORD has made;
    let us rejoice and be glad in it.
(Psalm 118:1, 14-17, 19-24)

New Life

"For God so loved the world that he gave his only Son, so that everyone who believes in him may not perish but may have eternal life." **(John 3:16)**

Just as one man's trespass led to condemnation for all, so one man's act of righteousness leads to justification and life for all. For just as by the one man's disobedience the many were made sinners, so by the one man's obedience the many will be made righteous. **(Romans 5:18-19)**

We have been buried with him by baptism into death, so that, just as Christ was raised from the dead by the glory of the Father, so we too might walk in newness of life.

For if we have been united with him in a death like his,

we will certainly be united with him in a resurrection like his. We know that our old self was crucified with him so that the body of sin might be destroyed, and we might no longer be enslaved to sin. For whoever has died is freed from sin. But if we have died with Christ, we believe that we will also live with him. We know that Christ, being raised from the dead, will never die again; death no longer has dominion over him. The death he died, he died to sin, once for all; but the life he lives, he lives to God. **(Romans 6:4-10)**

"This is indeed the will of my Father, that all who see the Son and believe in him may have eternal life; and I will raise them up on the last day." **(John 6:40)**

Our paschal lamb, Christ, has been sacrificed. Therefore, let us celebrate the festival, not with the old yeast, the yeast of malice and evil, but with the unleavened bread of sincerity and truth. **(1 Corinthians 5:7-8)**

We have such a high priest, one who is seated at the right hand of the throne of the Majesty in the heavens, a minister in the sanctuary and the true tent that the Lord, and not any mortal, has set up. **(Hebrews 8:1-2)**

"The word is near you,
     on your lips and in your heart"
(that is, the word of faith that we proclaim); because if

you confess with your lips that Jesus is Lord and believe in your heart that God raised him from the dead, you will be saved. (**Romans 10:8-9**)

God raised him on the third day and allowed him to appear, not to all the people but to us who were chosen by God as witnesses, and who ate and drank with him after he rose from the dead. He commanded us to preach to the people and to testify that he is the one ordained by God as judge of the living and the dead. All the prophets testify about him that everyone who believes in him receives forgiveness of sins through his name. (**Acts 10:40-43**)

Alleluia!

Great and amazing are your deeds,
 Lord God the Almighty!
Just and true are your ways,
 King of the nations!
Lord, who will not fear
 and glorify your name?
For you alone are holy.
 All nations will come
 and worship before you,
for your judgments have been revealed.
(**Revelation 15:3-4**)

"See, the home of God is among mortals.
He will dwell with them as their God;
they will be his peoples,
and God himself will be with them;
he will wipe every tear from their eyes.
Death will be no more;
mourning and crying and pain will be no more,
for the first things have passed away. . . .
See, I am making all things new. . . .
It is done! I am the Alpha and the Omega, the beginning and the end. To the thirsty I will give water as a gift from the spring of the water of life. Those who conquer will inherit these things, and I will be their God and they will be my children." (**Revelation 21:3-7**)

Chapter 22 | *Pentecost*

[For additional prayers on the Holy Spirit, see Chapter 2 on the Sacrament of Confirmation.]

When you send forth your spirit, they are created;
    and you renew the face of the ground.
(Psalm 104:30)

The Promise of the Spirit

"Very truly, I tell you, no one can enter the kingdom of God without being born of water and Spirit. What is born of the flesh is flesh, and what is born of the Spirit is spirit. Do not be astonished that I said to you, 'You must be born from above.' The wind blows where it chooses, and you hear the sound of it, but you do not know where it comes from or where it goes. So it is with everyone who is born of the Spirit." (John 3:5-8)

"I tell you the truth: it is to your advantage that I go away, for if I do not go away, the Advocate will not come to you; but if I go, I will send him to you. And when he comes, he will prove the world wrong about sin and righteousness and judgment: about sin, because they do not believe in me; about righteousness, because I am going to the Father and you will see me no longer; about judgment, because the ruler of this world has been condemned.

"I still have many things to say to you, but you cannot bear them now. When the Spirit of truth comes, he will guide you into all the truth; for he will not speak on his own, but will speak whatever he hears, and he will declare to you the things that are to come. He will glorify me, because he will take what is mine and declare it to you." (John 16:7-14)

"You will receive power when the Holy Spirit has come upon you; and you will be my witnesses in Jerusalem, in all Judea and Samaria, and to the ends of the earth."
(**Acts 1:8**)

The Promise Fulfilled

When the day of Pentecost had come, they were all together in one place. And suddenly from heaven there came a sound like the rush of a violent wind, and it filled the entire house where they were sitting. Divided tongues, as of fire, appeared among them, and a tongue rested on each of them. All of them were filled with the Holy Spirit and began to speak in other languages, as the Spirit gave them ability. (**Acts 2:1-4**)

This is what was spoken through the prophet Joel:
  "In the last days it will be, God declares,
  that I will pour out my Spirit upon all flesh,
      and your sons and your daughters shall prophesy,
  and your young men shall see visions,
      and your old men shall dream dreams.
  Even upon my slaves, both men and women,
      in those days I will pour out my Spirit;
          and they shall prophesy.
  And I will show portents in the heaven above
      and signs on the earth below,

blood, and fire, and smoky mist.
The sun shall be turned to darkness
and the moon to blood,
before the coming of the Lord's great
and glorious day.
Then everyone who calls on the name of the Lord
shall be saved."
(**Acts 2:17-21**)

And because you are children, God has sent the Spirit of his Son into our hearts, crying, "Abba! Father!" So you are no longer a slave but a child, and if a child then also an heir, through God. (**Galatians 4:6-7**)

He saved us, not because of any works of righteousness that we had done, but according to his mercy, through the water of rebirth and renewal by the Holy Spirit. This Spirit he poured out on us richly through Jesus Christ our Savior, so that, having been justified by his grace, we might become heirs according to the hope of eternal life.
(**Titus 3:5-7**)

The Spirit and the bride say, "Come."
And let everyone who hears say, "Come."
And let everyone who is thirsty come.
Let anyone who wishes take the water of life as a gift.
(**Revelation 22:17**)